# The Minimum Wage

# Other Books in the Issues on Trial Series:

# The Minimum Wage

*Uma Kukathas, Book Editor*

**GREENHAVEN PRESS**
*A part of Gale, Cengage Learning*

Detroit • New York • San Francisco • New Haven, Conn • Waterville, Maine • London

Christine Nasso, *Publisher*
Elizabeth Des Chenes, *Managing Editor*

© 2010 Greenhaven Press, a part of Gale, Cengage Learning

*For more information, contact:*
Greenhaven Press
27500 Drake Rd.
Farmington Hills, MI 48331-3535
Or you can visit our Internet site at gale.cengage.com.

For product information and technology assistance, contact us at

Gale Customer Support, 1-800-877-4253
For permission to use material from this text or product, submit all requests online at
www.cengage.com/permissions

Further permissions questions can be emailed to permissionrequest@cengage.com

Articles in Greenhaven Press anthologies are often edited for length to meet page requirements. In addition, original titles of these works are changed to clearly present the main thesis and to explicitly indicate the author's opinion. Every effort is made to ensure that Greenhaven Press accurately reflects the original intent of the authors. Every effort has been made to trace the owners of copyrighted material.

Cover photograph reproduced by permission of Win McNamee/Getty Images.

**LIBRARY OF CONGRESS CATALOGING-IN-PUBLICATION DATA**

The minimum wage / Uma Kukathas, book editor.
   p. cm. -- (Issues on trial)
   Includes bibliographical references and index.
   ISBN-13: 978-0-7377-4491-0 (hardcover)
   1. Minimum wage--Law and legislation--United States--Cases--Juvenile literature. 2. Constitutional law--United States--Cases--Juvenile literature. I. Kukathas,
Uma.
   KF3490.M528 2009
   344.7301'23--dc22
                              2009026340

Printed in the United States of America
1 2 3 4 5 6 7 13 12 11 10 09

# Contents

## Chapter 1: Declaring Minimum Wage Laws a Violation of Liberty of Contract

## Chapter 2: Upholding the Constitutionality of Minimum Wage Legislation

## Chapter 3: Denying Fair Labor Standards and Upholding States' Rights

## Chapter 4: Federalizing the Minimum Wage

# Foreword

The U.S. courts have long served as a battleground for the most highly charged and contentious issues of the time. Divisive matters are often brought into the legal system by activists who feel strongly for their cause and demand an official resolution. Indeed, subjects that give rise to intense emotions or involve closely held religious or moral beliefs lay at the heart of the most polemical court rulings in history. One such case was *Brown v. Board of Education* (1954), which ended racial segregation in schools. Prior to *Brown*, the courts had held that blacks could be forced to use separate facilities as long as these facilities were equal to that of whites.

For years many groups had opposed segregation based on religious, moral, and legal grounds. Educators produced heartfelt testimony that segregated schooling greatly disadvantaged black children. They noted that in comparison to whites, blacks received a substandard education in deplorable conditions. Religious leaders such as Martin Luther King Jr. preached that the harsh treatment of blacks was immoral and unjust. Many involved in civil rights law, such as Thurgood Marshall, called for equal protection of all people under the law, as their study of the Constitution had indicated that segregation was illegal and un-American. Whatever their motivation for ending the practice, and despite the threats they received from segregationists, these ardent activists remained unwavering in their cause.

Those fighting against the integration of schools were mainly white southerners who did not believe that whites and blacks should intermingle. Blacks were subordinate to whites, they maintained, and society had to resist any attempt to break down strict color lines. Some white southerners charged that segregated schooling was *not* hindering blacks' education. For example, Virginia attorney general J. Lindsay Almond asserted, "With the help and the sympathy and the love and respect of the white people of the South, the colored man has risen under that educational process to a place of eminence and respect throughout the nation. It has served him well." So when the Supreme Court ruled against the segregationists in *Brown*, the South responded with vociferous cries of protest. Even government leaders criticized the decision. The governor of Arkansas, Orval Faubus, stated that he would not "be a party to any attempt to force acceptance of change to which the people are so overwhelmingly opposed." Indeed, resistance to integration was so great that when black students arrived at the formerly all-white Central High School in Arkansas, federal troops had to be dispatched to quell a threatening mob of protesters.

Nevertheless, the *Brown* decision was enforced and the South integrated its schools. In this instance, the Court, while not settling the issue to everyone's satisfaction, functioned as an instrument of progress by forcing a major social change. Historian David Halberstam observes that the *Brown* ruling "deprived segregationist practices of their moral legitimacy. . . . It was therefore perhaps the single most important moment of the decade, the moment that separated the old order from the new and helped create the tumultuous era just arriving." Considered one of the most important victories for civil rights, *Brown* paved the way for challenges to racial segregation in many areas, including on public buses and in restaurants.

In examining *Brown*, it becomes apparent that the courts play an influential role—and face an arduous challenge—in shaping the debate over emotionally charged social issues. Judges must balance competing interests, keeping in mind the high stakes and intense emotions on both sides. As exemplified by *Brown*, judicial decisions often upset the status quo and initiate significant changes in society. Greenhaven Press's Issues on Trial series captures the controversy surrounding influential court rulings and explores the social ramifications of such decisions from varying perspectives. Each anthology highlights one social issue—such as the death penalty, students' rights, or wartime civil liberties. Each volume then focuses on key historical and contemporary court cases that helped mold the issue as we know it today. The books include a compendium of primary sources—court rulings, dissents, and immediate reactions to the rulings—as well as secondary sources from experts in the field, people involved in the cases, legal analysts, and other commentators opining on the implications and legacy of the chosen cases. An annotated table of contents, an in-depth introduction, and prefaces that overview each case all provide context as readers delve into the topic at hand. To help students fully probe the subject, each volume contains book and periodical bibliographies, a comprehensive index, and a list of organizations to contact. With these features, the Issues on Trial series offers a well-rounded perspective on the courts' role in framing society's thorniest, most impassioned debates.

# Introduction

From the beginning of the Civil War to the early part of the twentieth century, the United States went through a major industrial expansion that brought broad social and economic changes. With these changes came increased concern over the working conditions of nonagricultural workers, many of whom were women and children. Conditions in workplaces such as factories altered long-standing views about the nature of work in general and employment contracts in particular. Marxists, Fabian socialists, political progressives, and religious reformers began to question the notion of "free contracts" between consenting partners, suggesting that employers had overwhelmingly greater power and workers little ability to bargain for wages in a free and equal manner. Opposition to what were seen as harmful or unjust working conditions found expression in state legislatures.

Between 1840 and 1920, states passed a host of maximum-hour and minimum-wage laws. Maximum-hour legislation came first, with New Hampshire (1847) and Pennsylvania (1848) leading the way. These early directives lacked force, however. In 1874 Massachusetts passed the first enforceable restriction on hours limiting the work week for women to sixty hours. By 1900, 26 percent of the states had maximum-hour laws covering women, children, and, in some cases, men. The Supreme Court's response was mixed. In *Holden v. Hardy* (1898) the Court upheld an eight-hour maximum for workmen in the hazardous industries of mining and smelting in Utah. In 1908 in *Muller v. Oregon*, the Supreme Court also upheld a maximum-hours law aimed at protecting the "health and morals" of women workers. In 1905, however, the Court ruled that a New York law limiting bakers' hours violated individual contracting rights extended under the Fourteenth Amendment's due process clause. This was the landmark case *Lochner v. New York*.

The line of reasoning in these cases seems to be that government has the right to use its "police powers" to interfere with employment contracts only when it is necessary to protect health and morals, or when one of the parties lacks the power to bargain on roughly equal footing. Women and children were deemed especially vulnerable to harm to their health and morals, and also to exploitation by unscrupulous employers. In addition, the *Lochner* ruling underscored the idea that it is the Court's duty to determine whether legislation is "a fair, reasonable and appropriate exercise of the police power of the State."

Minimum-wage legislation came later and met with less early success in the courts than maximum-hour laws. Massachusetts was the first state to pass a minimum-wage law (1912). The law required that a board be appointed to set a minimum wage for women but allowed for a subminimum wage to be paid to learners, children, and "slow" workers. By 1920, sixteen other states had passed minimum-wage laws.

The first such law to be scrutinized by the U.S. Supreme Court was Oregon's 1914 attempt to mandate a minimum wage for most women in the state. In *Setter v. O'Hara* (1917), the Court decided that Oregon's decree was a valid exercise of its police powers and did not intrude excessively on individual liberty in general or freedom of contract in particular. Six years later, however, in *Adkins v. Children's Hospital* (1923), the court expressed a much different opinion. Within four years *Adkins* was used to overturn ten of the twelve state minimum-wage laws still being enforced.

The controversy in *Adkins* involved a District of Columbia law requiring a minimum wage for women workers. The law was challenged on grounds it would cost hardworking employees their jobs and place too great a burden on employers. Such governmental interference, the plaintiff's lawyers contended, was a violation of Fifth Amendment guarantees of due process and thus an illegitimate extension of states' police powers. The Court agreed and ruled the D.C. restriction on women's wages unconstitutional. Women, the majority explained, had recently won the right to vote and thus no longer needed special protections in labor negotiations. Interestingly, what was seen by some as a blow to progressive economic reform was viewed by others as an advance in the cause of women's rights.

The stock market crash of 1929 and the subsequent depression paved the way for the election of Franklin D. Roosevelt to the presidency and generated increased popular and political support for economic regulation. The Supreme Court responded to these events and in 1937 upheld the validity of minimum-wage legislation in *West Coast Hotel Co. v. Parrish.* The case involved a 1913 Washington state minimum-wage law that had escaped the spate of post-*Adkins* nullifications in the 1920s. The case came to the Supreme Court after Elsie Parrish sued her employer for wages guaranteed under the law. Her employer, West Coast Hotel Company, argued that minimum-wage laws violated their freedom of contract guaranteed under the due process clause of the Fourteenth Amendment. They expected the Court to overturn Washington's law just as it had barred similar laws in the thirteen years since *Adkins.*

Justice Charles Evans Hughes, writing for the majority, did not dispute the similarity of Washington's law to other laws they had been overturned in light of *Adkins.* He argued, however, that *Adkins* deserved a second look because of the current economic circumstances and legislatures' persistent resolve to pass minimum-wage laws. Upon reexamination, he attacked the *Adkins* reasoning on all of its key points. Women, he said, were still in need of support in wage negotiations; there was no special distinction between maximum-hour laws and minimum-wage laws; and minimum-wage laws would not serve just to create an imbalance favoring employees instead of employers.

*West Coast Hotel Co. v. Parrish* provided further ammunition for those favoring economic regulation and the reconfiguration of the right to free contract. In 1938 Congress passed the Fair Labor Standards Act (FLSA), which established minimum-wage and maximum-hour requirements for all federal employees engaged in interstate commerce. Like much of the New Deal legislation, the FLSA expanded the commerce powers of the federal government to regulate business. Notably, the FLSA explicitly excluded state and local governments from its purview. In the 1940s wartime inflation made the specific wage requirements irrelevant. The next major round of amendments and debate began in 1961.

In 1961 the FLSA's reach was extended to cover public schools and hospitals, among other entities. In 1963 Congress passed the Equal Pay Act, which made it illegal for employers to pay workers different rates just because of their sex. Soon after, farmworkers and employees over age forty acquired increased federal protection. Many of these expansions were addressed, and then validated, by the Supreme Court in *Maryland v. Wirtz* (1968), in which the Court found that the FLSA as amended did indeed apply to state schools and hospitals. Then, in 1974, an FLSA amendment extended its coverage to all state and local workers who had previously been explicitly excluded from federal regulation. This move was seen by many as a clear violation of the Tenth Amendment protection of state sovereignty.

The objection to the 1974 extension of the FLSA reached the Court in the form of *National League of Cities v. Usery* (1976). The Court retreated from its endorsement in *Wirtz* and concluded that "insofar as the 1974 amendments operate directly to displace the States' abilities to structure employer-employee relationships in areas of traditional government functions ... they are not within the authority granted Congress by the Commerce Clause." After this ruling, many predicted further limits on legislative commerce powers. They were wrong. In *Garcia v. San Antonio Metropolitan Transit Authority* (1985) the Court reversed its 1976 decision. The reasoning was especially noteworthy. Instead of arguing that the Court had incorrectly distributed federal power to states in *National League of Cities*, Justice Harry Blackmun argued that any judicial attempt to draw a clean line between state interests and federal interest was futile. The balancing of state and federal interests should be left to the legislature. This view was strongly opposed as "irresponsible" by the four dissenting justices. Justice William Rehnquist for his part predicted that *Garcia* would soon be overruled.

While *Garcia* has not been reversed, the Court did move the balance of power back toward states in later cases (*New York v. United States* [1992] and *United States v. Lopez* [1995]), reasserting its authority to interpret constitutional limits on Congress's power to regulate interstate commerce. The Court's decisions since *National League of Cities* exhibit what Justice Sandra Day O'Connor has called its "unsteady path" with regard to Tenth Amendment issues.

The debate about the minimum wage continues, whether it is centered on Congress's power to regulate private transactions or on its power to control the economic affairs of state and local government. This anthology explores the debate by looking at four significant Supreme Court decisions related to the minimum wage in the United States: *Adkins v. Children's Hospital* (1923), *West Coast Hotel Co. v. Parrish* (1937), *National League of Cities v. Usery* (1976), and *Garcia v. San Antonio Metropolitan Transit Authority* (1985). In presenting the Supreme Court's decisions and dissenting views as well as commentary by legal experts on these cases, *Issues on Trial: The Minimum Wage* illustrates the likelihood that the precise balance point between federal, state, and private interests relating to the minimum wage will continue to shift, at least incrementally, with changes in U.S. society's values and economic prospects.

# CHAPTER 1

# Declaring Minimum Wage Laws a Violation of Liberty of Contract

# Case Overview

## *Adkins v. Children's Hospital* (1923)

On April 9, 1923, the U.S. Supreme Court decided in *Adkins v. Children's Hospital* that minimum wage laws for women are unconstitutional because they interfered with the freedom of contract guaranteed by the Fifth and Fourteenth Amendments.

*Adkins* came to the Supreme Court as a pair of cases brought against the District of Columbia Minimum Wage Board, directed by Jesse Adkins. Congress established the board in 1918 to "protect the women and minors of the District from conditions detrimental to their health and morals, resulting from wages that are inadequate to maintain decent standards of living." The legal cases originated after the board passed a requirement that women workers in restaurants and "mercantile establishments" be paid at least $16.50 per week.

In the first case, *Lyons v. Adkins*, 21-year-old Willie Lyons sued to prevent the board from enforcing its orders against her employer, the Congress Hall Hotel. She liked her job as an elevator operator, despite making only $35 a month plus two meals a day. If the board enforced its ruling, the hotel would fire her. In the second case, Children's Hospital of the District of Columbia sought an injunction to prevent the board from enforcing its minimum wage requirement. The hospital employed a large number of women in a variety of jobs; many of them earned less than $16.50 a week.

The primary legal question presented to the Court was whether a minimum wage law violated an individual's freedom of contract as guaranteed by the due process clauses of the Fifth and Fourteenth Amendments. Earlier cases had established that "employer and employee have equality of right, and any legislation that disturbs that equality is an arbitrary interference with the liberty of contract." Previous decisions had also placed certain limits on individual freedom.

Writing for the majority, Justice George Sutherland argued that minimum wage laws did not fall under any of the previously established justifications for limiting individual liberty. Further, he said, minimum wage laws give too much bargaining power to employees, destroying the condition of equality required for free contracting. He noted as well the danger in allowing Congress to interfere with free contracting; the power to set a minimum wage logically entails the power to set a maximum wage, he argued, which clearly oversteps constitutional protections of individual freedom.

In his dissenting opinion, William Howard Taft judged minimum wage laws to be equivalent to maximum hour laws, which were ruled constitutional to protect workers' health. He disagreed with Sutherland on whether low wages were a cause of poor health. In speaking to what Sutherland regarded as his most important point, Taft argued that employers clearly had the upper hand in negotiations with low-wage employees, who "are prone to accept pretty much anything that is offered." Finally, Taft argued that the path from minimum wage laws to a dangerous expansion of governmental power can be blocked by careful judicial reasoning.

Immediately after *Adkins*, union leaders railed against the Court, minimum-wage boards advised that states ignore the ruling, and some lawmakers suggested giving Congress power to overrule the Supreme Court. President Franklin Roosevelt's Depression-era New Deal legislation advanced the minimum-wage cause, with the Fair Labor Standards Act of 1938 requiring a minimum wage for all employees doing interstate business. The Supreme Court upheld the constitutionality of the act in 1941.

*Adkins* also played a significant role in the women's movement. While some advocates agreed with the Minimum Wage Board's judgment that women needed special protection, feminists who championed "equality, not protection" saw the assumption as deeply sexist and strongly opposed the law.

> "Freedom of contract is . . . the general
> rule and restraint the exception."

# Majority Opinion: Minimum Wage Law Is a Violation of Liberty of Contract

*George Sutherland*

*Appointed to the Supreme Court by President Warren G. Harding, George Sutherland served as an associate justice from 1922 to 1938. In the majority opinion in the case of* Adkins v. Children's Hospital *(1923), Sutherland maintained that a law establishing a minimum wage for women and children was unconstitutional. The issue in* Adkins *was a 1918 federal statute prohibiting women in the District of Columbia from working for less than the established minimum wage. The law was designed by authorities to "protect the health and morals of women from degrading living conditions." The Children's Hospital of the District of Columbia, which employed many women at wages below those established, sued on the grounds that the regulation violated liberty of contract guaranteed by the Fifth Amendment, as defined in* Lochner v. New York *(1905). Sutherland argues in this opinion that the federal statute violated liberty of contract, which stipulates that the government should not interfere with the constitutional right of individuals to contract with their employers concerning wages, hours, and working conditions. Further, according to Sutherland, women could not be subjected to a different regulation than men, and employers should not be saddled with the responsibility of their employees' well-being.*

George Sutherland, majority opinion, *Adkins v. Children's Hospital*, U.S. Supreme Court, 1923.

The question presented for determination by these appeals is the constitutionality of the Act of September 19, 1918, providing for the fixing of minimum wages for women and children in the District of Columbia.

The act provides for a board of three members, to be constituted, as far as practicable, so as to be equally representative of employers, employees and the public. . . .

[T]he purposes of the act are

> to protect the women and minors of the District from conditions detrimental to their health and morals, resulting from wages which are inadequate to maintain decent standards of living, and the Act in each of its provisions and in its entirety shall be interpreted to effectuate these purposes.

The appellee in the first case is a corporation maintaining a hospital for children in the District. It employs a large number of women in various capacities, with whom it had agreed upon rates of wages and compensation satisfactory to such employees, but which in some instances were less than the minimum wage fixed by an order of the board made in pursuance of the act. The women with whom appellee had so contracted were all of full age and under no legal disability. The instant [present] suit was brought by the appellee in the Supreme Court of the District to restrain the board from enforcing or attempting to enforce its order on the ground that the same was in contravention of the Constitution, and particularly the due process clause of the Fifth Amendment.

In the second case, the appellee, a woman twenty-one years of age, was employed by the Congress Hall Hotel Company as an elevator operator, at a salary of $35 per month and two meals a day. She alleges that the work was light and healthful, the hours short, with surroundings clean and moral, and that she was anxious to continue it for the compensation she was receiving, and that she did not earn more. Her services were satisfactory to the Hotel Company, and it would have been glad to retain her but was obliged to dispense with her services by reason of the order of the board and on account of the penalties prescribed by the act. The wages received by this appellee were the best she was able to obtain for any work she was capable of performing, and the enforcement of the order, she alleges, deprived her of such employment and wages. She further averred that she could not secure any other position at which she could make a living, with good physical and moral surroundings, and earn as good wages, and that she was desirous of continuing and would continue the employment but for the order of the board. An injunction was prayed [asked for] as in the other case.

## Lower Court Findings

The Supreme Court of the District denied the injunction and dismissed the bill in each case. Upon appeal, the Court of Appeals, by a majority, first affirmed and subsequently, on a rehearing, reversed the trial court. Upon the first argument, a justice of the District Supreme Court was called in to take the place of one of the Appellate Court justices, who was ill. Application for rehearing was made and, by the court as thus constituted, was denied. Subsequently, and during the term, a rehearing was granted by an order concurred in by two of the Appellate Court justices, one being the justice whose place on the prior occasion had been filled by the Supreme Court member. Upon the rehearing thus granted, the Court of Appeals, rejecting the first opinion, held the act in question to be unconstitutional and reversed the decrees of the trial court. Thereupon the cases were remanded, and the trial court entered decrees in pursuance of the mandate, declaring the act in question to be unconstitutional and granting permanent injunctions. Appeals to the Court of Appeals followed, and the decrees of the trial court were affirmed. It is from these final decrees that the cases come here.

Upon this state of facts the jurisdiction of the lower court to grant a rehearing, after first denying it, is challenged. We do not deem it necessary to consider the matter farther than to say that we are here dealing with the second appeals, while the proceedings complained of occurred upon the first appeals. That the lower court could properly entertain the second appeals and decide the cases does not admit of doubt, and this the appellants virtually conceded by having themselves invoked the jurisdiction.

## Acts of Congress and the Constitution

We come then, at once, to the substantive question involved.

The judicial duty of passing upon the constitutionality of an act of Congress is one of great gravity and delicacy. The statute here in question has successfully borne the scrutiny of the legislative branch of the government, which, by enacting it, has affirmed its validity, and that determination must be given great weight. This Court, by an unbroken line of decisions from Chief Justice [John] Marshall to the present day, has steadily adhered to the rule that every possible presumption is in favor of the validity of an act of Congress until overcome beyond rational doubt. But if, by clear and indubitable demonstration, a statute be opposed to the Constitution, we have no choice but to say so. The Constitution, by its own terms, is the supreme law of the land, emanating from the people, the repository of ultimate sovereignty under our form of government. A congressional statute, on the other hand, is the act of an agency of this sovereign authority, and, if it conflict with the Constitution, must fall; for that which is not supreme must yield to that which is. To hold it invalid (if it be invalid) is a plain exercise of the judicial power—that power vested in courts to enable them to administer justice according to law. From the authority to ascertain and determine the law in a given case, there necessarily results, in case of conflict, the duty to declare and enforce the rule of the supreme law and reject that of an inferior act of legislation which, transcending the Constitution, is of no effect and binding on no one. This is not the exercise of a substantive power to review and nullify acts of Congress, for no such substantive power exists. It is simply a necessary concomitant of the power to hear and dispose of a case or controversy properly before the court, to the determination of which must be brought the test and measure of the law.

The statute now under consideration is attacked upon the ground that it authorizes an unconstitutional interference with the freedom of contract included within the guaranties or the due process clause of the Fifth Amendment. That the right to contract about one's affairs is a part of the liberty of the individual protected by this clause, is settled by the decisions of this court and is no longer open to question.... Within this liberty are contracts of employment of labor. In making such contracts, generally speaking, the parties have an equal right to obtain from each other the best terms they can as the result of private bargaining....

## Precedents

There is, of course, no such thing as absolute freedom of contract. It is subject to a great variety of restraints. But freedom of contract is, nevertheless, the general rule, and restraint the exception, and the exercise of legislative authority to abridge it can be justified only by the existence of exceptional circumstances. Whether these circumstances exist in the present case constitutes the question to be answered. It will be helpful to this end to review some of the decisions where the interference has been upheld and consider the grounds upon which they rest.

1. *Those dealing with statutes fixing rates and charges to be exacted by businesses impressed with a public interest.*
   There are many cases, but it is sufficient to cite *Munn v.*

*Illinois.* The power here rests upon the ground that, where property is devoted to a public use, the owner thereby, in effect, grants to the public an interest in the use which may be controlled by the public for the common good to the extent of the interest thus created. . . .

2. *Statutes relating to contracts for the performance of public work. Atkin v. Kansas; Helm v. McCall; Ellis v. United States.* These cases sustain such statutes as depending not upon the right to condition private contracts, but upon the right of the government to prescribe the conditions upon which it will permit work of a public character to be done for it, or, in the case of a State, for its municipalities. We may, therefore, in like manner, dismiss these decisions from consideration as inapplicable.

3. *Statutes prescribing the character, methods and time for payment of wages.* Under this head may be included *Mclean v. Arkansas*, sustaining a state statute requiring coal to be measured for payment of miners' wages before screening; *Knoxville Iron Co. v. Harbison*, sustaining a Tennessee statute requiring the redemption in cash of store orders issued in payment of wages; *Erie R.R. Co. v. Williams*, upholding a statute regulating the time within which wages shall be paid to employees in certain specified industries, and other cases sustaining statutes of like import and effect. In none of the statutes thus sustained was the liberty of employer or employee to fix the amount of wages the one was willing to pay and the other willing to receive interfered with. Their tendency and purpose was to prevent unfair and perhaps fraudulent methods in the payment of wages, and in no sense can they be said to be, or to furnish a precedent for, wage-fixing statutes.

4. *Statutes fixing hours of labor.* It is upon this class that the greatest emphasis is laid in argument. . . . In some

instances, the statute limited the hours of labor for men in certain occupations, and in others it was confined in its application to women. No statute has thus far been brought to the attention of this Court which by its terms, applied to all occupations. In *Holden v. Hardy*, the Court considered an act of the Utah legislature, restricting the hours of labor in mines and smelters. This statute was sustained as a legitimate exercise of the police power on the ground that the legislature had determined that these particular employments, when too long pursued, were injurious to the health of the employees, and that, as there were reasonable grounds for supporting this determination on the part of the legislature, its decision in that respect was beyond the reviewing power of the federal courts.

That this constituted the basis of the decision is emphasized by the subsequent decision in *Lochner v. New York*, reviewing a state statute which restricted the employment of all persons in bakeries to ten hours in any one day. The Court referred to *Holden v. Hardy*, and, declaring it to be inapplicable, held the statute unconstitutional as an unreasonable, unnecessary and arbitrary interference with the liberty of contract, and therefore void under the Constitution. . . .

Subsequent cases in this Court have been distinguished from that decision, but the principles therein stated have never been disapproved. . . .

## Regulating Hours vs. Fixing Wages

The essential characteristics of the statute now under consideration, which differentiate it from the laws fixing hours of labor, will be made to appear as we proceed. It is sufficient now to point out that the latter, as well as the statutes mentioned under paragraph (3), deal with incidents of the employment having no necessary effect upon the heart of the contract, that is, the amount of wages to be paid and received. A law forbidding work to continue beyond a given number of hours leaves the parties free to contract about wages, and thereby equalize whatever additional burdens may be imposed upon the employer as a result of the restrictions as to hours, by an adjustment in respect of the amount of wages. Enough has been said to show that the authority to fix hours of labor cannot be exercised except in respect of those occupations where work of long continued duration is detrimental to health. This Court has been careful, in every case where the question has been raised, to place its decision upon this limited authority of the legislature to regulate hours of labor and to disclaim any purpose to uphold the legislation as fixing wages, thus recognizing an essential difference between the two. It seems plain that these decisions afford no real support for any form of law establishing minimum wages.

If now, in the light furnished by the foregoing exceptions to the general rule forbidding legislative interference with freedom of contract, we examine and analyze the statute in question, we shall see that it differs from them in every material respect. It is not a law dealing with any business charged with a public interest or with public work, or to meet and tide over a temporary emergency. It has nothing to do with the character, methods or periods of wage payments. It does not prescribe hours of labor or conditions under which labor is to be done. It is not for the protection of persons under legal disability or for the prevention of fraud. It is simply and exclusively a price-fixing law, confined to adult women (for we are not now considering the provisions relating to minors), who are legally as capable of contracting for themselves as men. It forbids two parties having lawful capacity—under penalties as to the employer—to freely contract with one another in respect of the price for which one shall render service to the other in a purely private employment where both are willing, perhaps anxious, to agree, even though the consequence may be to oblige one to surrender a desirable engagement and the other to dispense with the services of a desirable employee. The price fixed by the board need have no relation to the capacity or earning power of the employee, the number of hours which may happen to constitute the day's work, the character of the place where the work is to be done, or the circumstances or surroundings of the employment; and, while it has no other basis to support its validity than the assumed necessities of the employee, it takes no account of any independent resources she may have. It is based wholly on the opinions of the members of the board and their advisers—perhaps an average of their opinions, if they do not precisely agree—as to what will be necessary to provide a living for a woman, keep her in health and preserve her morals. It applies to any and every occupation in the District, without regard to its nature or the character of the work.

## To Maintain Health and Protect Morals

The standard furnished by the statute for the guidance of the board is so vague as to be impossible of practical application with any reasonable degree of accuracy. What is sufficient to supply the necessary cost of living for a woman worker and maintain her in good health and protect her morals is obviously not a precise or unvarying sum—not even approximately so. The amount will depend upon a variety of circumstances: the individual temperament, habits of thrift, care, ability to buy necessaries intelligently, and whether the woman live alone or with her family. To those who practice economy, a given sum will afford comfort, while to those of contrary habit the same sum will be wholly inadequate. The cooperative economics of the family group are not taken into account though they constitute an important consideration in estimating the cost of living, for it is obvious that the individual expense will be less in the case of a member of a family than in the case of one living alone. The relation between earnings and morals is not capable of standardization. It cannot be shown that well paid women safeguard their morals more carefully than those who are poorly paid. Morality rests upon other considerations than wages, and there is, certainly, no such prevalent connection between the two as to justify a broad attempt to adjust the latter with reference to the former. As a means of safeguarding morals the attempted classification in our opinion, is without reasonable basis. No distinction can be made between women who work for others and those who do not; nor is there ground for distinction between women and men, for, certainly, if women require a minimum wage to preserve their morals men require it to preserve their honesty. For these reasons, and others which might be stated, the inquiry in respect of the necessary cost of living and of the income necessary to preserve health and morals, presents an individual, and not a composite, question, and must be answered for each individual considered by herself, and not by a general formula prescribed by a statutory bureau.

This uncertainty of the statutory standard is demonstrated by a consideration of certain orders of the board already made. These orders fix the sum to be paid to a woman employed in a place where food is served or in a mercantile establishment, at $16.50 per week; in a printing establishment, at $15.50 per week, and in a laundry, at $15 per week, with a provision reducing this to $9 in the case of a beginner. If a woman employed to serve food requires a minimum of $16.50 per week, it is hard to understand how the same woman working in a printing establishment or in a laundry is to get on with an income lessened by from $1 to $7.50 per week. The board probably found it impossible to follow the indefinite standard of the statute, and brought other and different factors into the problem, and this goes far in the direction of demonstrating the fatal uncertainty of the act, an infirmity which, in our opinion, plainly exists.

## Employers and Standards of Efficiency

The law takes account of the necessities of only one party to the contract. It ignores the necessities of the employer by compelling him to pay not less than a certain sum not only whether the employee is capable of earning it, but irrespective of the ability of his business to sustain the burden, generously leaving him, of course, the privilege of abandoning his business as an alternative for going on at a loss. Within the limits of the minimum sum, he is precluded, under penalty of fine and imprisonment, from adjusting compensation to the differing merits of his employees. It compels him to pay at least the sum fixed in any event, because the employee needs it, but requires no service of equivalent value from the employee. It therefore undertakes to solve but one-half of the problem. The other half is the establishment of a corresponding standard of efficiency, and this forms no part of the policy of the legislation, although in practice the former half without the latter must lead to ultimate failure, in accordance with the inexorable law that no one can continue indefinitely to take out more than he puts in without ultimately exhausting the supply. The law is not confined to the great and powerful employers, but embraces those whose bargaining power may be as weak as that of the employee. It takes no account of periods of stress and business depression, of crippling losses, which may leave the employer himself without adequate means of livelihood. To the extent that the sum fixed exceeds the fair value of the services rendered, it amounts to a compulsory exaction from the employer for the support of a partially indigent person, for whose condition there rests upon him no peculiar responsibility, and therefore, in effect, arbitrarily shifts to his shoulders a burden which, if it belongs to anybody, belongs to society as a whole.

## Paying for Work Performed

The feature of this statute which, perhaps more than any other, puts upon it the stamp of invalidity is that it exacts from the employer an arbitrary payment for a purpose and upon a basis having no causal connection with his business, or the contract or the work the employee engages to do. The declared basis, as already pointed out, is not the value of the service rendered, but the extraneous circumstance that the employee needs to get a prescribed sum of money, to insure her subsistence, health and morals. The ethical right of every worker, man or woman, to a living wage may be conceded. One of the declared and important purposes of trade organizations is to secure it. And with that principle, and with every legitimate effort to realize it in fact, no one can quarrel; but the fallacy of the proposed method of attaining it is that it assumes that every employer is bound at all events to furnish it. The moral requirement implicit in every contract of employment, *viz.* [namely], that the amount to be paid and the service to be rendered shall bear to each other some relation of just equivalence, is completely ignored. The necessities of the employee are alone considered, and these arise outside of the employment, are the same when there is no employment, and as great in one occupation as in another. Certainly the employer, by paying a fair equivalent for the service rendered, though not sufficient to support the employee, has neither caused nor contributed to her poverty. On the contrary, to the extent of what he pays, he has relieved it. In principle, there can be no difference between the case of selling labor and the case of selling goods. If one goes to the butcher, the baker or grocer to buy food, he is morally entitled to obtain the worth of his money, but he is not entitled to more. If what he gets is worth what he pays, he is not justified in demanding more simply because he needs more, and the shopkeeper, having dealt fairly and honestly in that transaction, is not concerned in any peculiar sense with the question of his customer's necessities. Should a statute undertake to vest in a commission power to determine the quantity of food necessary for individual support and require the shopkeeper, if he sell to the individual at all, to furnish that quantity at not more than a fixed maximum, it would undoubtedly fall before the constitutional test. The fallacy of any argument in support of the validity of such a statute would be quickly exposed. The argument in support of that now being considered is equally fallacious, though the weakness of it may not be so plain. A statute requiring an employer to pay in money, to pay at prescribed and regular intervals, to pay the value of the services rendered, even to pay with fair relation to the extent of the benefit obtained from the service, would be understandable. But a statute which prescribes payment without regard to any of these things and solely with relation to circumstances apart from the contract of employment, the business affected by it and the work done under it, is so clearly the product of a naked, arbitrary exercise of power that it cannot be allowed to stand under the Constitution of the United States.

## Arguments Justifying Minimum Wage

We are asked, upon the one hand, to consider the fact that several States have adopted similar statutes, and we are invited, upon the other hand, to give weight to the fact that three times as many States, presumably as well informed and as anxious to promote the health and morals of their people, have refrained from enacting such legislation. We have also been furnished with a large number of printed opinions approving the policy of the minimum wage, and our own reading has disclosed a large number to the contrary. These are all proper enough for the consideration of the lawmaking bodies, since their tendency is to establish the desirability or undesirability of the legislation; but they reflect no legitimate light upon the question of its validity, and that is what we are called upon to decide. The elucidation of that question cannot be aided by counting heads.

It is said that great benefits have resulted from the operation of such statutes, not alone in the District of Columbia, but in the several States where they have been in force. A mass of reports, opinions of special observers and students of the subject, and the like has been brought before us in support of this statement, all of which we have found interesting but only mildly persuasive. That the earnings of women now are greater than they were formerly, and that conditions affecting women have become better in other respects, may be conceded, but convincing indications of the logical relation of these desirable changes to the law in question are significantly lacking. They may be, and quite probably are, due to other causes. We cannot close our eyes to the notorious fact that earnings everywhere in all occupations have greatly increased—not alone in States where the minimum wage law obtains, but in the country generally—quite as much or more among men as among women and in occupations outside the reach of the law as in those governed by it. No real test of the economic value of the law can be had during periods of maximum employment, when general causes keep wages up to or above the minimum; that will come in periods of depression and struggle for employment, when the efficient will be employed at the minimum rate, while the less capable may not be employed at all.

Finally, it may be said that if, in the interest of the public welfare, the police power may be invoked to justify the fixing of a minimum wage, it may, when the public welfare is thought to require it, be invoked to justify a maximum wage. The power to fix high wages connotes, by like course of reasoning, the power to fix low wages. If, in the face of the guaranties of the Fifth Amendment, this form of legislation shall be legally justified, the field for the operation of the police power will have been widened to a great and dangerous degree. If, for example, in the opinion of future lawmakers, wages in the building trades shall become so high as to preclude people of ordinary means from building and owning homes, an authority which sustains the minimum wage will be invoked to support a maximum wage for building laborers and artisans, and the same argument which has been here urged to strip the employer of his constitutional liberty of contract in one direction will be utilized to strip the employee of his constitutional liberty of contract in the opposite direction. A wrong decision does not end with itself: it is a precedent, and, with the swing of sentiment, its bad influence may run from one extremity of the arc to the other.

It has been said that legislation of the kind now under review is required in the interest of social justice, for whose ends freedom of contract may lawfully be subjected to restraint. The liberty of the individual to do as he pleases, even in innocent matters, is not absolute. It must frequently yield to the common good, and the line beyond which the power of interference may not be pressed is neither definite nor unalterable, but may be made to move, within limits not well defined, with changing need and circumstance. Any attempt to fix a rigid boundary would be unwise, as well as futile. But, nevertheless, there are limits to the power, and when these have been passed, it becomes the plain duty of the courts in the proper exercise of their authority to so declare. To sustain the individual freedom of action contemplated by the Constitution is not to strike down the common good, but to exalt it, for surely the good of society as a whole cannot be better served than the preservation against arbitrary restraint of the liberties of its constituent members.

It follows from what has been said that the act in question passes the limit prescribed by the Constitution, and, accordingly, the decrees of the court below are

*Affirmed.*

*"It is not the function of this Court to hold congressional acts invalid simply because they are passed to carry out economic views which the Court believes to be unwise or unsound."*

# Dissenting Opinion: Lawmakers Can and Do Place Restraints on Contracts

## William Howard Taft

*William Howard Taft was the twenty-seventh president of the United States, from 1909 to 1913. He was appointed to the Supreme Court under Warren G. Harding and served as chief justice from 1921 to 1930. In the following excerpt from his dissent in* Adkins v. Children's Hospital, *Taft takes issue with the idea accepted by the majority that a federal statute imposing a minimum wage for women and children in the District of Columbia violates the Constitution. Taft criticizes the majority for essentially substituting in their decision their economic policy preferences for that of the legislature. He disagrees with the Court that upholding the law would violate liberty of contract and extend the police power of the state, and he argues that a reasonable exercise of this power is meant to protect certain classes of society. Taft stresses that wages are no less a component in a contract than hours, and he cites decisions from past cases in which the Court allowed the terms of employment contracts to be curtailed for a variety of reasons.*

William Howard Taft, dissenting opinion, *Adkins v. Children's Hospital*, U.S. Supreme Court, 1923.

I regret much to differ from the Court in these cases.

The boundary of the police power beyond which its exercise becomes an invasion of the guaranty of liberty under the Fifth and Fourteenth Amendments to the Constitution is not easy to mark. Our Court has been laboriously engaged in pricking out a line in successive cases. We must be careful, it seems to me, to follow that line as well as we can and not to depart from it by suggesting a distinction that is formal, rather than real.

## Not the Court's Function

Legislatures, in limiting freedom of contract between employee and employer by a minimum wage, proceed on the assumption that employees, in the class receiving least pay, are not upon a full level of equality of choice with their employer, and, in their necessitous circumstances, are prone to accept pretty much anything that is offered. They are peculiarly subject to the overreaching of the harsh and greedy employer. The evils of the sweating system [which gave rise to the term *sweatshop*] and of the long hours and low wages which are characteristic of it are well known. Now I agree that it is a disputable question in the field of political economy how far a statutory requirement of maximum hours or minimum wages may be a useful remedy for these evils, and whether it may not make the case of the oppressed employee worse than it was before. But it is not the function of this Court to hold congressional acts invalid simply because they are passed to carry out economic views which the Court believes to be unwise or unsound.

Legislatures which adopt a requirement of maximum hours or minimum wages may be presumed to believe that, when sweating employers [sweatshop owners] are prevented from paying unduly low wages by positive law, they will continue their business, abating that part of their profits, which were wrung from the necessities of their employees, and will concede the better terms required by the law, and that, while in individual cases hardship may result, the restriction will enure [become an advantage] to the benefit of the general class of employees in whose interest the law is passed, and so to that of the community at large.

The right of the legislature under the Fifth and Fourteenth Amendments to limit the hours of employment on the score of the health of the employee, it seems to me, has been firmly established. As to that, one would think, the line had been pricked out so that it has become a well formulated rule. In *Holden v. Hardy*, it was applied to miners and rested on the unfavorable environment of employment in mining and smelting. In *Lochner v. New York*, it was held that restricting those employed in bakeries to ten hours a day was an arbitrary and invalid interference with the liberty of contract secured by the Fourteenth Amendment. Then followed a number of cases, beginning with *Muller v. Oregon*, sustaining the validity of a limit on maximum hours of labor for women, to which I shall hereafter allude, and, following these cases, came *Bunting v. Oregon*. In that case, this Court sustained a law limiting the hours of labor of any person, whether man or woman, working in any mill, factory or manufacturing establishment to ten hours a day with a proviso as to further hours to which I shall hereafter advert. The law covered the whole field of industrial employment, and certainly covered the case of persons employed in bakeries. Yet the opinion in the *Bunting* case does not mention the *Lochner* case. No one can suggest any constitutional distinction between employment in a bakery and one in any other kind of a manufacturing establishment which should make a limit of hours in the one invalid and the same limit in the other permissible. It is impossible for me to reconcile the *Bunting* case and the *Lochner* case, and I have always supposed that the *Lochner* case was thus overruled *sub silentio* ["under silence"; i.e., tacitly]. Yet the opinion of the

Court herein in support of its conclusion quotes from the opinion in the *Lochner* case as one which has been sometimes distinguished but never overruled. Certainly there was no attempt to distinguish it in the *Bunting* case.

## Wages and Hours Equally Important

However, the opinion herein does not overrule the *Bunting* case in express terms, and therefore I assume that the conclusion in this case rests on the distinction between a minimum of wages and a maximum of hours in the limiting of liberty to contract. I regret to be at variance with the Court as to the substance of this distinction. In absolute freedom of contract, the one term is as important as the other, for both enter equally into the consideration given and received, a restriction as to one is not any greater, in essence, than the other, and is of the same kind. One is the multiplier, and the other the multiplicand.

If it be said that long hours of labor have a more direct effect upon the health of the employee than the low wage, there is very respectable authority from close observers, disclosed in the record and in the literature on the subject quoted at length in the briefs, that they are equally harmful in this regard. Congress took this view, and we cannot say it was not warranted in so doing.

With deference to the very able opinion of the Court and my brethren who concur in it, it appears to me to exaggerate the importance of the wage term of the contract of employment as more inviolate than its other terms. Its conclusion seems influenced by the fear that the concession of the power to impose a minimum wage must carry with it a concession of the power to fix a maximum wage. This, I submit, is a *non sequitur* [something that does not logically follow]. A line of distinction like the one under discussion in this case is, as the opinion elsewhere admits, a matter of degree and practical experience, and not of pure logic. Certainly the wide difference between prescribing a minimum wage and a maximum wage could, as a matter of degree and experience, be easily affirmed.

Moreover, there are decisions by this Court which have sustained legislative limitations in respect to the wage term in contracts of employment. In *McLean v. Arkansas*, it was held within legislative power to make it unlawful to estimate the graduated pay of miners by weight after screening the coal. In *Knoxville Iron Co. v. Harbison*, it was held that store orders issued for wages must be redeemable in cash. In *Patterson v. Bark Eudora*, a law forbidding the payment of wages in advance was held valid. A like case is *Strathearn S.S. Co. v. Dillon*. While these did not impose a minimum on wages, they did take away from the employee the freedom to agree as to how they should be fixed, in what medium they should be paid, and when they should be paid, all features that might affect the amount or the mode of enjoyment of them. The first two really rested on the advantage the employer had in dealing with the employee. The third was deemed a proper curtailment of a sailor's right of contract in his own interest because of his proneness to squander his wages in port before sailing. In *Bunting v. Oregon*, employees in a mill, factory or manufacturing establishment were required, if they worked over ten hours a day, to accept for the three additional hours permitted not less than fifty percent more than their usual wage. This was sustained as a mild penalty imposed on the employer to enforce the limitation as to hours; but it necessarily curtailed the employee's freedom to contract to work for the wages he saw fit to accept during those three hours. I do not feel, therefore, that, either on the basis of reason, experience or authority, the boundary of the police power should be drawn to include maximum hours and exclude a minimum wage.

## Women and Work

Without, however, expressing an opinion that a minimum wage limitation can be enacted for adult men, it is enough to say that the case before us involves only the application of the minimum wage to women. If I am right in thinking that the legislature can find as much support in experience for the view that a sweating wage has as great and as direct a tendency to bring about an injury to the health and morals of workers, as for the view that long hours injure their health, then I respectfully submit that *Muller v. Oregon* [1908] controls this case. The law which was there sustained forbade the employment of any female in any mechanical establishment or factory or laundry for more than ten hours. This covered a pretty wide field in women's work, and it would not seem that any sound distinction between that case and this can be built up on the fact that the law before us applies to all occupations of women, with power in the board to make certain exceptions. Mr. Justice [David J.] Brewer, who spoke for the Court in *Muller v. Oregon*, based its conclusion on the natural limit to women's physical strength and the likelihood that long hours would therefore injure her health, and we have had since a series of cases which may be said to have established a rule of decision. *Riley v. Massachusetts, Miller v. Wilson, Bosley v. McLaughlin*. The cases covered restrictions in wide and varying fields of employment, and in the later cases, it will be found that the objection to the particular law was based not on the ground that it had general application, but because it left out some employments.

I am not sure from a reading of the opinion whether the Court thinks the authority of *Muller v. Oregon* is shaken by the adoption of the Nineteenth Amendment. The Nineteenth Amendment did not change the physical strength or limitations of women upon which the decision in *Muller v. Oregon* rests. The Amendment did give women political power, and makes more certain that legislative provisions for their protection will be in accord with their interests as they see them. But I don't think we are warranted in varying constitutional construction based on physical differences between men and women, because of the Amendment.

> *"Minimum-wage legislation is now un-constitutional, not because the Constitution makes it so ... but because it chanced not to come before a particular Supreme Court bench."*

# The *Adkins* Ruling Was Based on the Justices' Personal Views Rather than on Constitutionality

*Thomas Reed Powell*

*Thomas Reed Powell was a constitutional lawyer and political scientist who taught for twenty-five years at Harvard Law School. In the following selection, he argues that there is no answer in the U.S. Constitution regarding whether an employer should pay a wage that can maintain an employee who is voluntarily in his or her service. He focuses his comments on the case of* Adkins v. Children's Hospital, *in which the hospital argued that a law stipulating the minimum it could pay its female employees was unconstitutional. Powell reviews the history of the legislation and demonstrates that in the lower courts a large majority of judges thought that minimum wage laws were in fact constitutional. But when the question reached the Supreme Court, he points out, there happened to be more judges on the bench who were politically and ideologically opposed to such economic policies. Thus, Powell contends, the decision of the majority striking down minimum wage legislation was not based on an interpretation of the Constitution but on the justices' personal views.*

Thomas Reed Powell, "The Judiciality of Minimum Wage Legislation," *Harvard Law Review*, vol. 37, March 1924, pp. 545–73. Reproduced by permission.

Minimum-wage legislation has been of two main kinds. One is the Massachusetts variety which vests a commission with power to make inquiries and publish results. Employers are exposed to public knowledge of the wages paid and are thereby subjected to public censure or public praise. Sentiments of decency or of vanity may move the niggardly [stingy] to mend their ways, but the recalcitrant are left free to bargain as they can and will. The other type of legislation adds physical to moral force. A commission is authorized to discover and to declare the minimum cost of decent subsistence and on this basis to prescribe the minimum wage that may be paid to women and minors. Employment at less than the prescribed wage subjects the employer to punishment. While the variations in the wages fixed by various boards for various employments indicate that the cost of living is not always the sole criterion of the boards' determinations, there has been no judicial adjudication that their prescriptions have exceeded the cost of decent living. The constitutional issue raised by such compulsory legislation is therefore whether an employer may be compelled to pay the cost of maintaining the employee whose full services he voluntarily uses in the conduct of his enterprise.

## No Constitutional Answer

This constitutional question finds no answer in the Constitution. While the legislation, like substantially all legislation and all law, involves a deprivation of liberty or property, such deprivation is constitutionally innocuous unless it is "without due process of law." The Constitution does not define due process of law. The task of definition is committed to the judges. They have recognized that definition is impossible. They have told us that instead of definition they will employ a process of "judicial inclusion and exclusion," and give us the reasons. These reasons cannot come from the Constitution. They come from the judges. The law of constitutional due process is therefore as much judge-made law as any common law is judge-made law. Until some due-process issue is authoritatively settled, one who would make a constitutional prophecy or a constitutional argument should be familiar with the outlook and the temper of the judges by whom the issue is to be decided. In cases of any considerable novelty, few reasons can be so compelling as to meet with universal acceptance. The determination of closely-controverted constitutional issues depends, therefore, in large part upon the composition of the court of last resort at the particular time when the issue comes before it.

Nowhere does this analysis find firmer confirmation than in the history of judicial decisions on the constitutionality of minimum-wage legislation. The question first came before the Oregon court in 1914, and in two decisions seven judges declared themselves in favor of the legislation and none was opposed. The Oregon case went to the Supreme Court of the United States, and in 1917 the decree of the state court was sustained by a vote of four to four. Mr. Justice [Louis] Brandeis, having been of counsel, did not sit. His general outlook on what is called social legislation is so well known that there can be no doubt that, had he not been of counsel, he would have voted in favor of the law. In that event, the consequent five-to-four vote almost certainly would have established the constitutionality of such legislation against subsequent attack in the federal courts. Though conceivably a favorable decision might later have been overruled by a differently composed Supreme Court, the experience is that police issues of this general character are finally settled by such favorable decision. A four-to-four vote, however, settles nothing, except that the particular decision below is not reversed. After this tie vote, the constitutional issue still remained an open one. A prophet would be confident that if the same Supreme Court bench had the question to decide in a case in which Mr. Justice Brandeis should sit, the answer would be in favor of the legislation. By reason of this confidence, he might add to it the further confidence that the objectors to the legislation would not again bring the issue to the Supreme Court until its personnel had changed. Such turned out to be the fact. Four changes in the Supreme Court had taken place before the issue again came before it.

## History of Minimum Wage Legislation

In the meantime four other courts had passed upon the question. Two decisions of the Minnesota Supreme Court in 1917 and 1920 record six judges in favor of the legislation and none opposed. An Arkansas decision of 1917 sustained the legislation by a vote of four to one, though one of the majority refrained from dissent only because he thought that the legislation was entitled to the benefit of the Supreme Court tie until it was broken. Two decisions of the Supreme Court of Washington in 1918 and 1920 add eleven judges to those in favor of the legislation and none to those opposed. Thus the compulsory minimum-wage legislation of the states of Oregon, Minnesota, Arkansas, and Washington was thought constitutional by twenty-seven judges of the courts of those states and unconstitutional by only two judges, three of the four courts being unanimously in favor of the statutes.

Then came the anomalous somersault in the case before the Court of Appeals of the District of Columbia. This involved the act of Congress applicable to the District. On the first hearing Mr. Justice [Charles] Robb was unable to sit because of illness. Under statutory authority the other two Justices designated Mr. Justice [Wendell] Stafford of the Supreme Court of the District to sit in his place. The decision, on June 6, 1921, was two to one in favor of the statute. Chief Justice [Joseph] Smyth and Mr. Justice Stafford were in favor; Mr. Justice [Josiah] Van Orsdel was opposed. Motions for a rehearing were denied on June 22 of the same year. Three days later, Mr. Justice Robb, who had now recovered, wrote the

Chief Justice that he was considering an application for a rehearing. On July 1 he wrote that he had decided to vote for a rehearing and had so notified counsel and Mr. Justice Van Orsdel. Later Justices Robb and Van Orsdel instructed the clerk to enter an order granting a rehearing. The Chief Justice dissented. The case was reargued on February 14, 1921, and decided on November 6, 1922. The vote was two to one against the statute. Chief Justice Smyth in dissenting severely scored the method by which a rehearing was obtained. Thus those who sat in the two hearings in the District Court of Appeals were divided two to two. Summarizing the votes outside of the United States Supreme Court, we have twenty-nine judges thinking compulsory minimum-wage legislation not wanting in due process as against four judges thinking the contrary.

The District of Columbia adverse decision was appealed to the United States Supreme Court where it was argued on March 14, 1923, and decided on April 9, 1923, in *Adkins v. Children's Hospital.* The dates of the several proceedings in the District of Columbia case from its initiation to its final disposition in the Supreme Court are significant, for, as will later appear, the unconstitutionality of minimum-wage legislation has been dictated by the calendar rather than by the Constitution. The Supreme Court decision annulled the act of Congress by a vote of five to three. Mr. Justice Brandeis, . . . did not sit, notwithstanding the fact that technically he was eligible since his disqualification was confined to the Oregon litigation in which he had been of counsel. The opinion of the Court was written by Mr. Justice [George] Sutherland and concurred in by Justices [Joseph] McKenna, [Willis] Van Devanter, [James] McReynolds and [Pierce] Butler. Chief Justice [William Howard] Taft wrote a dissenting opinion in which Mr. Justice [Edward T.] Sanford concurred. Mr. Justice [Oliver Wendell] Holmes wrote an additional dissenting opinion. Adding these Supreme Court votes to the votes in the lower courts, we have a total of thirty-two judges voting in favor of the constitutionality of minimum-wage legislation and nine judges voting against it.

## Timing of *Adkins*

Now for the importance of the time when the question reached the Supreme Court. Three of the five Justices who voted against the legislation in 1923 were on the bench in 1917 when the Supreme Court was divided four to four. These were Justices McKenna, Van Devanter, and McReynolds. We may be confident, therefore, that they gave three of the four votes against the law in 1917. The other Justices sitting in 1917 were Chief Justice [Edward Douglass] White and Justices Holmes, [William] Day, [Mahlon] Pitney, and [John] Clarke. Since Mr. Justice Holmes dissented in 1923, we know that he voted for the law in 1917. Followers of Supreme Court divisions can be certain also that Mr. Justice Clarke was on the same side. This confines the surmise as to the fourth Justice against the law in 1917 to Chief Justice White and Justices Day and Pitney. The evidence of other divisions of opinion points almost conclusively to Chief Justice White as the fourth in opposition. He had been more consistently with Justices Van Devanter and McReynolds against extensions of the police power than had either Mr. Justice Day or Mr. Justice Pitney. In writing the opinion sustaining the constitutionality of the Adamson Law, he made a distinction between prescribing wages after the parties have failed to agree and prescribing wages in conjunction with forbidding or restricting an agreement, thus carefully differentiating minimum-wage legislation from the Adamson Law. Mr. Rome G. Brown, one of the counsel before the Supreme Court in the first minimum-wage case, picks Chief Justice White as one of the four opposed to the legislation. It seems, therefore, as safe a guess as any guess can be, that in 1917 Chief Justice White voted against minimum-wage legislation and Justices Day and Pitney voted in favor of it. Certainly three of these four Justices were in favor of the legislation and only one opposed, so that these votes added to the others already counted make a judicial majority of thirty-five to ten in favor, with the participating Supreme Court Justices divided six to six and a non-participating Justice known to be in favor.

## Make-up of the Bench

The bench sitting in 1917 continued until the end of the October term of 1920. During the October term of 1921 the only change was that of Chief Justice Taft in place of Chief Justice White. If our guess as to Chief Justice White is correct, the Supreme Court from October, 1921, to June, 1922, contained six Justices who thought minimum-wage legislation constitutional. One of these was Mr. Justice Brandeis who doubtless would have refrained from sitting then as he did in 1923. The others were Chief Justice Taft and Justices Holmes, Day, Pitney and Clarke. If, therefore, any state case or the District of Columbia case had been argued before and decided by the Supreme Court between November, 1921, and June, 1922, the decision would, in all probability, have been five to three in favor of minimum-wage legislation. Even if the surmise as to Chief Justice White were incorrect, and either Mr. Justice Day or Mr. Justice Pitney were opposed to the legislation, the vote would have been four to four, with Chief Justice Taft, Justices Holmes and Clarke, and either Mr. Justice Day or Mr. Justice Pitney in favor. This would have sustained the state decisions and the first District of Columbia decision had Mr. Justice Robb not intervened to bring about a rehearing. That intervention, be it noted, set aside a decision rendered on June 6, 1921, and postponed the ultimate decision in the District of Columbia Court of Appeals until November 6, 1922. The appeal from this decision reached the Supreme Court for argument in March, 1923, and was decided less than a month later. Thus the earlier 1921 District of Columbia decision might have reached the Supreme Court for adjudication some time before June, 1922. If, therefore, Mr. Justice Robb had sat at the first hearing and the decision had then been against the act of Congress, the appeal might have been decided by the Supreme Court before June, 1922, when there were certainly only four Justices of the Supreme Court opposed to the legislation and, in all probability, only three opposed to it. Thus the state laws would surely have been saved for the time from annulment, and almost certainly both state and national legislation would have been sustained by a decision that would have been accepted as settling the issue forever. So, for a second time, the course of constitutional principles was changed by circumstances peculiar to an individual judge: first, because Mr. Justice Brandeis chanced to have been of counsel at an earlier stage of the Oregon case; and, secondly, because Mr. Justice Robb of the District of Columbia Court of Appeals was indisposed when the act of Congress first came before that court for consideration.

Before the District of Columbia case came on for argument before the Supreme Court, there had intervened three further changes in the composition of that body, all due to resignations of sitting Justices. Mr. Justice Clarke was succeeded by Mr. Justice Sutherland; Mr. Justice Day, by Mr. Justice Butler; and Mr. Justice Pitney, by Mr. Justice Sanford. By these changes either a possible tie vote of four to four or, more probably, a five-to-three vote in favor of minimum-wage legislation was turned into a five-to-three vote against it. It would, of course, be idle to speculate as to whether the new appointees to the bench would have been the same had the resigning Justices been different or had their resignations been in a different order. It can, however, hardly be attributed to anything but chance that the resignations after June, 1922, were of two or three Justices favoring minimum-wage legislation and that the new appointments added two Justices opposing it. It cannot well be attributed to any assumed leanings of the appointing authority, since the four new Justices appointed by President [Warren G.] Harding were evenly divided on the issue. The political complexion of the bench at the time is of no significance. It is doubtless idle, too, to speculate as to whether Justices Sutherland and Butler might have voted differently had the question not come before them until they were further away from their days of legislation and of advocacy, and therefore perhaps more impregnated with the professed traditions of judicial tolerance in passing upon the constitutionality of legislation under the amorphous caution of the due-process clauses. Suffice it to say that minimum-wage legislation is now unconstitutional, not because the Constitution makes it so, not because its economic results or its economic propensities would move a majority of judges to think it so, but because it chanced not to come before a particular Supreme Court bench which could not muster a majority against it and chanced to be presented at the succeeding term when the requisite, but no more than requisite, majority was sitting. In the words of the poet, it was not the Constitution but "a measureless malfeasance which obscurely willed it thus"—the malfeasance of chance and of the calendar.

Such is the only possible realistic account of the reason why minimum-wage legislation is unconstitutional. Literary interpretation of the Constitution has nothing whatever to do with it. Neither legal learning nor economic exposition can explain it. Arguments *pro* and arguments *contra* have no compelling inherent power. The issue was determined not by the arguments but by the arbiters. The majority of the arbiters on the state courts favored the legislation, but under our constitutional system the majority of the arbiters on the Supreme Court have the determining voice. The unanimous vote of the electors of a state through solemn amendment of the constitution of the state could not reverse the vote of five members of the Supreme Court of the United States. This can be done only by the Supreme Court itself or by amendment of the Constitution of the United States.

# *Adkins* Addressed the Constitutionality of the Inequality of Women

## Joan G. Zimmerman

*Joan G. Zimmerman is a historian and scholar who has written on American women and legal and constitutional history. In the following viewpoint, she discusses the impact of* Adkins v. Children's Hospital *on early efforts at drafting an equal rights amendment (ERA). In* Adkins, *a hospital argued that the law requiring it to pay its female employees a minimum wage violated their right to liberty of contract. Zimmerman demonstrates how the minimum wage became the battleground for different views on how to determine the rights of women. Two women fighting for gender equality, Florence Kelley and Alice Paul, who held very different positions on how to best secure greater rights for women, took particular interest in the* Adkins *case because it signaled how the courts would view the ideas of women's dependence or independence. When the Court found that women were no less subject to freedom of contract than men, it distressed feminists like Kelley, who sought equality of social conditions for women. Paul, on the other hand, welcomed the decision because she believed according equality a formal legal status would empower women. Zimmerman shows how the decision handed*

Joan G. Zimmerman, "The Jurisprudence of Equality: The Women's Minimum Wage, The First Equal Rights Amendment, and *Adkins v. Children's Hospital*, 1905–1923," *Journal of American History*, vol. 76, June 1991, pp. 188–225. Copyright © 1991 by the Organization of American Historians. Reproduced by permission.

*down by the conservative Court ultimately reshaped women's rights and the formulation of the ERA.*

The debate over the language of the first ERA [Equal Rights Amendment], which went through over thirty-five drafts, intersected with proposals for statutory reforms designed to improve working conditions for women in the labor force. Advocates of such hours and wage legislation for women had developed strategies to evade the barriers created by legal for-malism—particularly the courts' interpretation of the Four-teenth Amendment's due process clause—and to establish a new basis for talk of rights. As an outspoken and effective proponent of protective labor legislation for women, [social reformer] Florence Kelley sought to redefine rights and the meaning of equality for women in an industrial economy. Her arguments raised questions about how useful an emphasis on individualism and equality with men was for women seeking to articulate their political and social goals. After 1920, con-flicts among women themselves over the meaning of their new republican citizenship were drawn into and became part of the jurisprudential debate over formalism and instrumen-talism. Whether talk of rights among women would challenge legal barriers or be co-opted by those with power would be decided in the first women's minimum wage case after the Nineteenth Amendment. The directors of the Children's Hos-pital in Washington, D.C., challenged the power of the District of Columbia minimum wage board (chaired by Jesse Adkins) to set wages for the hospital's women employees. Drawing on conceptions of liberty in the legal formalist tradition, the hospital's lawyers argued that the 1918 law establishing the board conflicted with the Fourteenth Amendment's guarantees because it deprived both the hospital and its employees of lib-erty of contract without due process of law. That case, *Adkins v. Children's Hospital,* not only reconstructed rights talk but also showed that at least for the leaders of the National Woman's Party (NWP), legal formalism was not a barrier, but an avenue to desired reforms.

## Using the Law for Social Reform

As reformers adjusted their laws and proposals to accommodate legal rules and approaches, they necessarily created new arguments to defend them. Those new arguments did not always reflect the original views of the reformers. In the 1890s, for example, Kelley focused on regulations for sweatshops; by 1921 Kelley had developed more elaborate arguments that focused on women's maternal functions. Kelley was interested in getting specific laws sustained by the courts, and her arguments addressed the specific issues pertinent to each type of protective law. Kelley relied on older common law views since she realized that judges usually did not wish to inaugurate radical shifts away from established precedents. The best example of Kelley's understanding of the legal barriers to protective legislation and her resulting emphasis on women's physical weakness is the Sheppard-Towner Maternity and Infancy-Protection Act of 1921. Kelley considered this act, which was based on the spending power of Congress, the high point of her career. In her defense of the Sheppard-Towner Act, Kelley frequently referred to women's maternal functions, and historians have often quoted her remarks to argue that Kelley believed in women's inequality. Yet Kelley's defense of the minimum wage, which was at issue in the *Adkins* case, did not rely on women's maternal functions. Instead, she focused on responding to the courts' interpretation of the due process clause of the Fourteenth Amendment.

The litigation that culminated in the *Adkins* decision altered the course of social reform, recast women's claims to constitutional rights, and propelled Kelley and [suffragist Alice] Paul toward different, incompatible kinds of arguments. The close relationship between the *Adkins* decision and the emergence of the ERA—a relationship clearly understood by participants in the debate over equality—illustrates how specific reforms can intersect with legal doctrines and principles. In broader terms, the jurisprudential divisions that helped polarize the women's movement may also illuminate other struggles for reform in the Progressive Era.

## Kelley and Paul Clash

Rather than being the basis for an empty liberty to contract for one's labor, the due process clause, in Kelley's view, was an invitation to promote the orderly processes of the law. Those orderly processes of statute making would lead to more ethical gains, which in turn formed the basis of a cooperative commonwealth. Yet within a few months, Kelley's plan for ethical gains became hopelessly entangled in the debate over the drafting of the first Equal Rights Amendment.

While Florence Kelley had seen suffrage as only one of several possible advances for women, Alice Paul, head of the newly reorganized National Woman's Party, viewed the ratification [in 1920] of the Nineteenth Amendment [guaranteeing American women the right to vote] as the end of one era in the struggle for women's rights and the beginning of a drive to enact full equality between men and women. The timing of her efforts to construct an equal rights amendment between 1921 and 1923 forced her to confront the program for ethical gains Kelley was pursuing. In particular, the women's minimum wage became the battleground between Kelley and her protectionist allies on one hand and Paul and the National Woman's Party on the other. The litigation over the District of Columbia minimum wage act, which began in 1920, would not only determine the victor in the first round of a continuing struggle over the meaning of rights and equality for women but would also test the limits of the dependent woman theory.

Paul was much less familiar than Kelley with legal thinking and the jurisprudential context. Paul's initial efforts to free married women from common law constraints made her increasingly wary of legislation that relied on a theory of women's dependence. Throughout 1921, the dramatic shifts in the language of Paul's drafts of the ERA reflected her reliance on and confrontation with several lawyers and legal scholars, many of whom were hostile to the new sociological jurisprudence. During the struggle to draft the first ERA, Paul consistently embraced the nineteenth-century heritage of women's rights as it had been developed by Susan B. Anthony and Elizabeth Cady Stanton. Her understanding of that heritage led Paul to insist on women's individualism and equality with men. How these apparently timeless demands were interpreted and refashioned in the legal environment of the early 1920s was one of the ironies of Paul's seemingly radical insistence on an ERA for women. . . .

## The Supreme Court on Equality

In April 1923 in the case of *Adkins v. Children's Hospital*, the United States Supreme Court struck down the District of Columbia law authorizing the establishment of minimum wages for women. The five-to-three majority opinion in the *Adkins* case not only joined women's legal equality with formalism but also undermined Kelley's vision of ethical gains in a revived Republic. In the opinion, [Justice George] Sutherland used the Nineteenth Amendment to show that women were no longer dependents and that they could now be treated as equals to men. There was no longer any reason to exempt them from the rule of liberty of contract.

> We cannot accept the doctrine that women of mature age, *sui juris* [capable of making one's own legal decisions], require or may be subjected to restrictions upon their liberty of contract which could not lawfully be imposed in the case of men under similar circumstances. To do so would be to

ignore all the implications to be drawn from the usage, by which woman is accorded emancipation from the old doctrine that she must be given special protection or be subjected to special restraint in her contractual and civil relationships.

Sutherland pointed out that the minimum wage law had not balanced means and ends. He saw no connection between morals and health on one hand and a minimum wage on the other. . . . Sutherland's opinion demonstrated that the idea of liberty of contract made famous in *Lochner* [*v. New York* (1905)] not only survived but applied with full force to women who worked for wages. Kelley's dependent woman theory as it applied to minimum wage laws had been undone. Justice Charles Robb quickly sent Sutherland a note of congratulations on the *Adkins* decision.

When [legal scholar and later Supreme Court justice Felix] Frankfurter read Sutherland's opinion, he immediately detected Paul's fingerprints in the treatment of the implications of the Nineteenth Amendment. He wired Kelley:

> Confidential: Most ominous part of the opinion is suggestion that Muller doctrine [of *Muller v. Oregon* ] has been supplanted by nineteenth amendment. . . . Upshot would be adoption Alice Paul theory of constitutional law plus invalidity of legislation affecting industrial relations of either men or women.

The deed was done. Paul now had the sanction of the Supreme Court for her view of equality. In fact, Sutherland's termination of the dependent woman theory had gone almost too far. His broad claims for the Nineteenth Amendment's emancipation of women had almost undermined the need for the ERA.

## Questioning Sutherland's Judgment

Other reactions to *Adkins* suggest that there were suspicions about Sutherland's discussion of equality for women. For example, [appellant] Jesse Adkins wrote, "The opinion was written so soon after the argument and is one of a number of opinions written during the same opinion week by Justice Sutherland, I cannot believe that he had time to fully digest the subject." Oregon attorney William Brewster reacted with annoyance: "I was greatly interested to see, among other things, that Sutherland accepted and used the language of the appellee's brief even in those places where I thought the Messrs. Ellis [appellee's attorneys] were using stump speech and jury addressing arguments."

Kelley was dismayed and bitter. She reflected on "that stagnant period from 1895–1908," from the *Ritchie* [*v. the People* (1895)] decision in Illinois to the *Muller* decision, when the courts had applied the liberty-of-contract doctrine to women. Now, the *Adkins* decision might signal a return to that dark period. Recalling her plan for ethical gains through the orderly processes of the law, Kelley assessed the revival of the old meaning of due process in *Adkins*.

> Under the Fifth and Fourteenth Amendments of the federal Constitution as now interpreted by the court, it is idle to seek to assure by orderly processes of legislation, to wage-earning men, women, or children, life, liberty or the pursuit of happiness. This decision fills those words with the bitterest and most cruel mockery. . . . Under the pressure of competition in American industry at this time, it establishes in the practical experience of the unorganized, the unskilled, the illiterate, the alien, and the industrially sub-normal women wage-earners, the constitutional right to starve. This is a new "Dred Scott" decision.

One of her supporters put it more succinctly: "The pendulum has come back."

## *Adkins* and the ERA

What was reaction to Kelley was new hope for Paul. Yet Paul did not openly boast about this victory. She simply repeated her position of October 1921 on labor legislation: the NWP took no stand on minimum wage legislation but insisted that all laws should apply to men and women alike. After the *Adkins* decision was announced in early April 1923, Paul stepped up her plan to introduce the ERA in Congress in December 1923.

While the *Adkins* decision paved the way for the ERA, several additional developments enabled Paul to write her own version of it. She had completed her legal studies, and she took the bar exam in June 1923. [NWP lawyer] Burnita Matthews was completing her research into state laws, and the party now had a better understanding of the implications of the amendment. Although state branches had succeeded in eliminating some minor discriminations in 1922 and 1923, their slow and erratic progress demonstrated a need for a national amendment. Paul planned to announce her new ERA in July 1923, at an outdoor pageant in Seneca Falls celebrating the seventy-fifth anniversary of the first women's rights convention [there]. The publicity for the pageant, she hoped, would launch a nationwide effort for passage of the ERA.

Without the help of any other lawyers, Paul drafted a simple, straightforward statement that said, "Men and women shall have Equal Rights throughout the United States and every place subject to its jurisdiction." Her clear, positive language belied the complicated twists and turns of the drafting process in 1921. There was no saving clause and no need to limit its intentions to the problems of married women. By early November, the party had lined up two legislators willing to introduce the Equal Rights Amendment when Congress convened in early December. They were Senator [Charles] Curtis, who would be Herbert Hoover's running mate in 1928, and Rep. Daniel Anthony, Susan B. Anthony's nephew. The long, confusing period of drafting the first ERA had finally ended, and the struggle over passage through Congress had begun.

Both Kelley and Paul had sought to improve the circumstances of women's lives by using the law as an instrument of change. The timing of their efforts drew their arguments over women's equality and rights into a vortex of conflicting views over approaches to jurisprudence. When Kelley found the formalist emphasis on liberty of contract anathema to her vision of social progress and legal reform, she developed one of the most ambitious theoretical and practical assaults on formalism of the Progressive Era. She had discovered that legal formalism, as the paradigm of conservative jurisprudence, could be evaded as long as women's interests were aligned with the public good. Yet her creation of a counterfiction showed that she could not entirely escape the tenets of formalism. Her emphasis on the common law view of women as dependents was one of the costs of seeking social change in a conservative legal environment. Her expansive view of rights in an industrial economy represented an attempt to capture the promise of life, liberty, and the pursuit of happiness for the powerless. In the most significant test of her ideas, the *Adkins* decision rejected her view of the law, equality, and the Republic and reclaimed talk of rights for employers and legal formalism in a free market economy.

## Sutherland Co-opts Paul's View

In later years, Matthews hailed Sutherland's words in the *Adkins* opinion as "the *Magna Charta* of women's rights:" The National Woman's Party adopted women's right to make their own contracts as the cornerstone of liberty for women. Paul's ambitious vision of women's complete equality with men in all social and legal relations had been reduced to a legal fiction. By formalizing Paul's talk of rights, Sutherland had co-opted Paul's view and narrowed it to serve the most conservative economic and legal interests. Her attempt to seek public power for women had shown that individualism and equality, rather than being timeless values, could be turned against women by conservative judges. Sutherland had joined the ERA with a nineteenth-century theory of economic individualism that would become increasingly outmoded even in the Supreme Court by the late 1930s. The NWP got what those with power wanted it to have.

How the *Adkins* decision reshaped rights talk among women themselves is an irony of the first postsuffrage struggle to redefine women's "proper position in society." Kelley understood how perverse the courts could be. "The definitions of 'equal rights' in the fourteenth and fifteenth [amendments] have been continuously injurious, first to the Negroes, and afterward to white women and children. I see no reason for expecting the Court to interpret fresh attempts to put political and social equality into the Constitution more favorably to women than they have done in the past." Kelley recognized that Americans disagreed about the meaning of equality. To one NWP member she wrote, "I am, for instance, entitled to interpret 'equality' as 'identical' just as you are entitled to interpret otherwise; and in the end, the Court may adopt a third interpretation wholly divergent from both. . . . And the root of the trouble all the time is the Courts." After the *Adkins* decision, Kelley added her most ambitious ethical gain to her list. "I shall strive to modernize the Court and the Constitution," she wrote. "My debates with the Woman's Party are one per cent against an Amendment which will never be adopted, and 99% for women judges and a responsible Court." Kelley had turned the formalist victory in *Adkins* into an example of sociological jurisprudence: pointing out that courts are as political as legislatures may always be the outsider's trump.

To women seeking access to power and control of legal definitions of women's rights after achieving the right to vote, the *Adkins* decision demonstrated the hazards a conservative legal environment posed. Legal requirements had forced both Kelley and Paul to frame their arguments about women's equality to conform to judicial expectations. As both compromised themselves, they drew further apart. The narrow judicial definition of women's rights that emerged from their struggle exacted heavy costs. By establishing a male standard that was itself based on a legal fiction, the *Adkins* opinion polarized the women's movement and limited the debate over equality. Kelley's imaginative vision of social reform and civic responsibility for women and for all groups in the Republic was lost not only to the women of the 1920s but also to the historians who have studied their debate. Long after the liberty-of-contract fiction dropped out of judicial discourse, the legacy of formalism persisted both in women's definition of equality as legal identity with men and in exaggerated defenses of protective legislation based on women's weaknesses. What had begun as an attempt to capture constitutional definitions of rights on behalf of women's interests and the interests of the Republic ended as a war of fictions.

> *"[Sutherland's] judgments were . . . part*
> *of the same moral and legal reasoning*
> *by which he measured any attempt,*
> *through the law, to restrict the freedom*
> *of individuals."*

# The *Adkins* Decision Was Not Based on Personal Prejudice

## Hadley Arkes

*Hadley Arkes is a conservative political scientist and the Edward N. Ney Professor of Jurisprudence and American Institutions at Amherst College. In the following excerpt from his full-length study of George Sutherland, he defends the justice from charges that in* Adkins v. Children's Hospital *his opinion was based not on the Constitution but on his personal prejudices. The case concerned a 1918 federal statute guaranteeing a minimum wage to women and children in the District of Columbia. Children's Hospital argued that forcing it to pay its female employees the minimum stipulated in the statute violated their constitutional rights guaranteed by the due process clause of the Fifth Amendment. Arkes contends that Sutherland rejected the notion of minimum wage legislation not because it conflicted with his own economic views, but because it restricted the freedom of individuals.*

As for [Justice George] Sutherland himself, he seemed to suffer no strain as he moved from the political arena to the more sedate setting, and the more scholarly life, of the

Hadley Arkes, "Figure in the Carpet," in *The Return of George Sutherland: Restoring a Jurisprudence of Natural Rights*. Princeton, NJ: Princeton University Press, 1994, pp. 20–22. Copyright © 1994 by Princeton University Press. Reprinted by permission of Princeton University Press.

Court. In his first season, the Court heard the argument in the Adkins cases, with Willie Lyons and the Children's Hospital contesting the law on minimum wages in the District of Columbia. That rather the unprepossessing case gave Sutherland the chance, almost at once, to show the reach and play of his mind. To adapt a phrase from [American author] Henry James, he was able to put his hand to this case in such a way as to "grasp his warrant" as a judge. The legislation in the District of Columbia was regarded as one of the more "advanced" measures of legislation struck off at the time. It sprung from the genius of the cleverest young professors of law, who were alert to the new possibilities for curing, through the edicts of law, the shortcomings of the economy. The law was defended in a brief written by Felix Frankfurter of the Harvard Law School, and the project was sustained by the most "progressive" opinion of the day. Under the statute, a board was constituted with the mandate to stipulate the precise wage, in any occupation, that would "supply the necessary cost of living to . . . women workers to maintain them in good health and to protect their morals." Evidently, the board understood the connection between morality and wages in the most calibrated way, for it was able to divine, with an astonishing particularity, that a woman working in a mercantile establishment required a wage of $16.50 per week to sustain her health, while a beginner in a laundry could apparently support herself and her morals with a more modest provision of $9 per week.

## Sutherland's Philosophic Reflex

We shall have the occasion, presently, to look closely again at the reasoning in this case and that massive missing of the point staged by the critics of the Court, namely, that Sutherland and his colleagues had struck down this statute because the policy did not accord with their prejudices, or their "predilections," about the way in which the "economy" ought to be arranged. I will try to show there was nothing in Sutherland's opinion that touched remotely on theories of the economy. Nor was the decision woven out of reasoning that was discernibly "economic." What was at work, rather, in Sutherland was a sound, philosophic reflex, which made him suspicious of theories of "determinism." In this case, that suspicion expressed itself in a certain skepticism that the drafters of the bill had access to any intelligible standard that could churn out for them the precise wages that were "right" to pay in all varieties of jobs, from a saleswoman at Garfinckel's department store to an assistant in a laundry.

As Sutherland went on to settle the groundwork of this judgment, he explained, in terms quite striking to people with some experience in the world, just what was wrong with policies that sought to fix, by statute, the level of wages and prices. It was not that these policies failed to "work." Sutherland would say nothing bearing on the utility of these measures. What he had to say on the subject, he said in principle, in terms that reached the moral grounds of any act that would claim the name of law.

## A Model of Force and Clarity

As I have suggested, Sutherland's reasoning in this case had nothing remotely to do with economics. His judgments were drawn from the same canons of reasoning that he employed when he considered restrictions on the press or the protection of defendants in a trial. They were part of the same moral and legal reasoning by which he measured any attempt, through the law, to restrict the freedom of individuals, in any of its dimensions. For Sutherland, it was part of that same discipline of reasoning that constituted the discipline of "constitutional" restraints on the exercise of authority. And this is the way that many judges at the time understood this early exercise by Sutherland in the craft of judging. From the Court of Appeals of the District of Columbia, Justice Charles Robb penned a short note bearing a concentrated admiration. "I've just finished reading," he said, "your opinion in the Minimum Wage Cases and I trust I may not be considered presumptuous in writing you how much it has impressed me. It is one of the best opinions I have ever read and its logic is irresistible."

[T]here was nothing hyperbolic or out of scale in this judgment. Sutherland's opinion was a model of force and clarity, and the body of his work would rank with the most compelling opinions written in the tradition of jurisprudence. Yet, fourteen years later, the overthrowing of this opinion was taken, by liberal writers and historians, as an event devoutly to be relished, the sign of a progressive turning in the jurisprudence of the Court. Over the dissent of Sutherland, the Court, in *West Coast Hotel v. Parrish*, upheld a state law on minimum wages for women, a law that should have been covered, without strain, by the rule of law articulated in *Adkins v. Children's Hospital*. This decision was part of a handful of decisions that seemed to mark the famous "switch in time that saved nine"— the willingness of the Court to give way, gradually, to Franklin Roosevelt and the political assault of the New Deal.

# CHAPTER 2

# Upholding the Constitutionality of Minimum Wage Legislation

# Case Overview

### *West Coast Hotel Co. v. Parrish* (1937)

In 1913 the state of Washington passed a law making it illegal "to employ women or minors . . . under conditions of labor detrimental to their health or morals" or offer wages that are "not adequate for their maintenance." In 1936 Elsie Parrish used this law to sue her employer, West Coast Hotel, for failing to pay her what the law required at the time. The hotel pointed out that the Supreme Court had declared minimum-wage laws unconstitutional thirteen years earlier, in *Adkins v. Children's Hospital*.

In *Adkins*, the Supreme Court concluded that the due process clause of the Fifth Amendment bars government from setting *arbitrary* limits on employer-employee contracting. The Court had earlier decided that a limiting law could be justified if it protected workers or the public from harm. However, since there was no measurable connection between low wages and poor "health or morals," wage restrictions could not be justified. Further, minimum wage laws would allow unproductive workers to claim wages they did not earn. The *Adkins* Court argued as well that laws offering special protections to women were no longer needed since women had gained the right to vote and could now protect their interests through the political process.

Reversing a position it had held for thirteen years, the Supreme Court declared Washington's minimum wage law valid. *West Coast Hotel v. Parrish* won in a five-to-four decision, with Justice Owen Roberts switching alliances and voting against the four conservative justices with whom he had consistently sided on other recent labor issues. Arguing for the majority, Justice Charles Evans Hughes declared that times had changed and that the Court's reasoning in *Adkins* was mistaken.

Women, he maintained, still needed special protection because they were physically weaker and society may limit a woman's freedom "to preserve the strength and vigor of the race." He dismissed the claim that low wages were no threat to health and found the *Adkins* Court inconsistent and arbitrary in allowing maximum-hour laws (to protect health) but not minimum-wage laws. Finally, Hughes pointed out that Washington's law required a board to set a rate of pay that was "fair" to both parties, thus preventing unscrupulous workers from exploiting their employers. He concluded that the law did not violate the Fourteenth Amendment's due process clause because it was designed to accomplish a "proper legislative purpose," and was not arbitrary.

Justice George Sutherland in his dissent took the majority to task for not following a clear precedent. "If *Adkins* was properly decided," Sutherland wrote, "it necessarily follows that the Washington statute is invalid." Sutherland also rejected the idea that women needed special protection, arguing that they should not be put in different classes than men in respect of their legal right to make contracts or to compete with men.

The Court's decision took place during a time of social anxiety and political pressure. The Depression had left many in dire economic circumstances. President Franklin D. Roosevelt, recently reelected, had been critical of the Court's opposition to his social welfare programs, chiding those standing in the way of his New Deal policies. He had gone so far as to propose to Congress a reorganization of the federal judiciary, allowing him to appoint six additional justices more amendable to his economic plans. After *Parrish*, Roosevelt's "court-packing" plan lost support. There was widespread speculation that Justice Roberts switched alliances because of political pressure, and the popular slogan used to describe the event was "the switch in time that saved nine." It is now known that the justices voted on *Parrish* before Roosevelt's bill was introduced, but there is still speculation about what went on behind the scenes and why Roberts switched positions. Whatever the role of politics in the case, it is certain that *West Coast Hotel Co. v. Parrish* signaled greater Supreme Court deference to economic regulation, ushering in the first federal minimum wage standard in 1938.

> *"The Constitution does not speak of freedom of contract. It speaks of liberty and prohibits the deprivation of liberty without due process of law."*

# Majority Opinion: The Constitution Does Not Speak of Freedom of Contract

*Charles Evans Hughes*

*Charles Evan Hughes served as the Republican governor of New York (1907–1910) before being appointed to the Supreme Court in 1910 by President William Howard Taft. He resigned from the Court in 1916 to run for president. After his defeat he returned to the private practice of law before being appointed secretary of state under Warren G. Harding. Herbert Hoover appointed him chief justice of the United States in 1930. Hughes wrote and delivered the majority opinion in the 1937 case of* West Coast Hotel Co. v. Parrish, *overturning the* Adkins *decision of 1923 and ruling that the Constitution permits the restriction of liberty of contract by state law where such restriction protects the community, health, and safety of vulnerable groups. The appellee in the case was Elsie Parrish, a chambermaid who brought suit against her employer to recover the difference between the wages paid her and the minimum wage legislated by the state of Washington. In deciding whether the minimum wage statute should be regarded as constitutional, Hughes reexamines the* Adkins v. Children's Hospital *decision. He argues that the Constitution*

Charles Evans Hughes, majority opinion, *West Coast Hotel Co. v. Parrish*, U.S. Supreme Court, 1937.

*does not protect freedom of contract (the basis of the* Adkins *decision) but rather prohibits the deprivation of liberty without due process of law.*

This case presents the question of the constitutional validity of the minimum wage law of the State of Washington.

The Act, entitled "Minimum Wages for Women," authorizes the fixing of minimum wages for women and minors. . . .

## Reexamining *Adkins*

The appellant conducts a hotel. The appellee, Elsie Parrish, was employed as a chambermaid and (with her husband) brought this suit to recover the difference between the wages paid her and the minimum wage fixed pursuant to the state law. The minimum wage was $14.50 per week of 48 hours. The appellant challenged the act as repugnant to the due process clause of the Fourteenth Amendment of the Constitution of the United States. . . .

The appellant relies upon the decision of this Court in *Adkins v. Children's Hospital*, 261 U.S. 525, which held invalid the District of Columbia Minimum Wage Act, which was attacked under the due process clause of the Fifth Amendment. On the argument at bar, counsel for the appellees attempted to distinguish the *Adkins* case upon the ground that the appellee was employed in a hotel, and that the business of an innkeeper was affected with a public interest. That effort at distinction is obviously futile, as it appears that, in one of the cases ruled by the *Adkins* opinion, the employee was a woman employed as an elevator operator in a hotel. . . .

The Supreme Court of Washington has upheld the minimum wage statute of that State. It has decided that the statute is a reasonable exercise of the police power of the State. In reaching that conclusion, the state court has invoked principles long established by this Court in the application of the Fourteenth Amendment. The state court has refused to regard the decision in the *Adkins* case as determinative, and has pointed to our decisions both before and since that case as justifying its position. We are of the opinion that this ruling of the state court demands on our part a reexamination of the *Adkins* case. The importance of the question, in which many States having similar laws are concerned, the close division by which the decision in the *Adkins* case was reached, and the economic conditions which have supervened, and in the light of which the reasonableness of the exercise of the protective power of the State must be considered, make it not only appropriate, but we think imperative, that, in deciding the present case, the subject should receive fresh consideration. . . .

## What Is Freedom of Contract?

The principle which must control our decision is not in doubt. The constitutional provision invoked is the due process clause of the Fourteenth Amendment, governing the States, as the due process clause invoked in the *Adkins* case governed Congress. In each case, the violation alleged by those attacking minimum wage regulation for women is deprivation of freedom of contract. What is this freedom? The Constitution does not speak of freedom of contract. It speaks of liberty and prohibits the deprivation of liberty without due process of law. In prohibiting that deprivation, the Constitution does not recognize an absolute and uncontrollable liberty. Liberty in each of its phases has its history and connotation. But the liberty safeguarded is liberty in a social organization which requires the protection of law against the evils which menace the health, safety, morals and welfare of the people. Liberty under the Constitution is thus necessarily subject to the restraints of due process, and regulation which is reasonable in relation to its subject and is adopted in the interests of the community is due process. . . .

This power under the Constitution to restrict freedom of contract has had many illustrations. That it may be exercised in the public interest with respect to contracts between employer and employee is undeniable. Thus, statutes have been sustained limiting employment in underground mines and smelters to eight hours a day (*Holden v. Hardy*); in requiring redemption in cash of store orders or other evidences of indebtedness issued in the payment of wages (*Knoxville Iron Co. v. Harbison*); in forbidding the payment of seamen's wages in advance (*Patterson v. Bark Eudora*); in making it unlawful to contract to pay miners employed at quantity rates upon the basis of screened coal instead of the weight of the coal as originally produced in the mine (*McLean v. Arkansas*); in prohibiting contracts limiting liability for injuries to employees (*Chicago, B. & Q. R. Co. v. McGuire*); in limiting hours of work of employees in manufacturing establishments (*Bunting v. Oregon*), and in maintaining workmen's compensation laws (*New York Central R. Co. v. White; Mountain Timber Co. v. Washington*). In dealing with the relation of employer and employed, the legislature has necessarily a wide field of discretion in order that there may be suitable protection of health and safety, and that peace and good order may be promoted through regulations designed to insure wholesome conditions of work and freedom from oppression.

The point that has been strongly stressed that adult employees should be deemed competent to make their own contracts was decisively met nearly forty years ago in *Holden v. Hardy, supra* [as mentioned above], where we pointed out the inequality in the footing of the parties. . . .

We think that the views thus expressed are sound, and that the decision in the *Adkins* case was a departure from the true application of the principles governing the regulation by the State of the relation of employer and employed. Those principles have been reenforced by our subsequent decisions. Thus, in *Radice v. New York*, we sustained the New York statute which restricted the employment of women in restaurants at night. In *O'Gorman & Young v. Hartford Fire Insurance Co.*, which upheld an act regulating the commissions of insurance agents, we pointed to the presumption of the constitutionality of a statute dealing with a subject within the scope of the police power and to the absence of any factual foundation of record for deciding that the limits of power had been transcended. . . .

## Public Interest in a Living Wage

With full recognition of the earnestness and vigor which characterize the prevailing opinion in the *Adkins* case, we find it impossible to reconcile that ruling with these well considered declarations. What can be closer to the public interest than the health of women and their protection from unscrupulous and overreaching employers? And if the protection of women is a legitimate end of the exercise of state power, how can it be said that the requirement of the payment of a minimum wage fairly fixed in order to meet the very necessities of existence is not an admissible means to that end? The legislature of the State was clearly entitled to consider the situation of women in employment, the fact that they are in the class receiving the least pay, that their bargaining power is relatively weak, and that they are the ready victims of those who would take advantage of their necessitous circumstances. The legislature was entitled to adopt measures to reduce the evils of the "sweating system," the exploiting of workers at wages so low as to be insufficient to meet the bare cost of living, thus making their very helplessness the occasion of a most injurious competition. The legislature had the right to consider that its minimum wage requirements would be an important aid in carrying out its policy of protection. The adoption of similar requirements by many States evidences a deep-seated conviction both as to the presence of the evil and as to the means adapted to check it. Legislative response to that conviction cannot be regarded as arbitrary or capricious, and that is all we have to decide. Even if the wisdom of the policy be regarded as debatable and its effects uncertain, still the legislature is entitled to its judgment.

There is an additional and compelling consideration which recent economic experience has brought into a strong light. The exploitation of a class of workers who are in an unequal position with respect to bargaining power, and are thus relatively defenceless against the denial of a living wage, is not only detrimental to their health and wellbeing, but casts a direct burden for their support upon the community. What these workers lose in wages, the taxpayers are called upon to pay. The bare cost of living must be met. We may take judicial notice of the unparalleled demands for relief which arose during the recent period of depression and still continue to an alarming extent despite the degree of economic recovery which has been achieved. It is unnecessary to cite official statistics to establish what is of common knowledge through the length and breadth of the land. While, in the instant [present] case, no factual brief has been presented, there is no reason to doubt that the State of Washington has encountered the same social problem that is present elsewhere. The community is not bound to provide what is, in effect, a subsidy for unconscionable employers. The community may direct its lawmaking power to correct the abuse which springs from their selfish disregard of the public interest. The argument that the legislation in question constitutes an arbitrary discrimination, because it does not extend to men, is unavailing. . . .

Our conclusion is that the case of *Adkins v. Children's Hospital, supra*, should be, and it is, overruled. The judgment of the Supreme Court of the State of Washington is *Affirmed*.

> *"The meaning of the Constitution does not change with the ebb and flow of economic events."*

# Dissenting Opinion: Constitutional Decisions Should Not Be Overturned Because of Historical Circumstances

## George Sutherland

*Appointed to the Supreme Court by President Warren G. Harding, George Sutherland served as an associate justice from 1922 to 1938. He had authored the 1923 majority opinion in* Adkins v. Children's Hospital, *which found that a minimum wage violated the constitutional guarantee of freedom of contract. In his dissent in* West Coast Hotel Co. v. Parrish, *which overturned* Adkins *in 1937, Sutherland reiterated his previous position that freedom of contract was the rule with few exceptions, and that the shift of the burden for the poor onto employers was an arbitrary and naked exercise of power. Sutherland insists that the meaning of the Constitution does not change along with changing economic conditions. He also maintains that treating men and women differently under the law amounts to arbitrary discrimination.*

The principles and authorities relied upon to sustain the judgment were considered in *Adkins v. Children's Hospital,* and *Morehead v. New York ex rel. Tipaldo,* and their lack of

George Sutherland, dissenting opinion, *West Coast Hotel Co. v. Parrish*, U.S. Supreme Court, 1937.

application to cases like the one in hand was pointed out. A sufficient answer to all that is now said will be found in the opinions of the court in those cases. Nevertheless, in the circumstances, it seems well to restate our reasons and conclusions.

Under our form of government, where the written Constitution, by its own terms, is the supreme law, some agency, of necessity, must have the power to say the final word as to the validity of a statute assailed as unconstitutional. The Constitution makes it clear that the power has been intrusted to this court when the question arises in a controversy within its jurisdiction, and, so long as the power remains there, its exercise cannot be avoided without betrayal of the trust.

It has been pointed out many times, as in the *Adkins* case, that this judicial duty is one of gravity and delicacy, and that rational doubts must be resolved in favor of the constitutionality of the statute. But whose doubts, and by whom resolved? Undoubtedly it is the duty of a member of the court, in the process of reaching a right conclusion, to give due weight to the opposing views of his associates; but, in the end, the question which he must answer is not whether such views seem sound to those who entertain them, but whether they convince him that the statute is constitutional or engender in his mind a rational doubt upon that issue. The oath which he takes as a judge is not a composite oath, but an individual one. And, in passing upon the validity of a statute, he discharges a duty imposed upon *him*, which cannot be consummated justly by an automatic acceptance of the views of others which have neither convinced, nor created a reasonable doubt in, his mind. If upon a question so important he thus surrender his deliberate judgment, he stands forsworn. He cannot subordinate his convictions to that extent and keep faith with his oath or retain his judicial and moral independence.

The suggestion that the only check upon the exercise of the judicial power, when properly invoked to declare a constitutional right superior to an unconstitutional statute, is the judge's own faculty of self-restraint is both ill-considered and mischievous. Self-restraint belongs in the domain of will, and not of judgment. The check upon the judge is that imposed by his oath of office, by the Constitution, and by his own conscientious and informed convictions, and since he has the duty to make up his own mind and adjudge accordingly, it is hard to see how there could be any other restraint. This court acts as a unit. It cannot act in any other way, and the majority (whether a bare majority or a majority of all but one of its members) therefore establishes the controlling rule as the decision of the court, binding, so long as it remains unchanged, equally upon those who disagree and upon those who subscribe to it. Otherwise, orderly administration of justice would cease. But it is the right of those in the minority to disagree, and sometimes, in matters of grave importance, their imperative duty to voice their disagreement at such length as the occasion demands—always, of course, in terms which, however forceful, do not offend the proprieties or impugn the good faith of those who think otherwise.

## New Economic Events

It is urged that the question involved should now receive fresh consideration, among other reasons, because of "the economic conditions which have supervened"; but the meaning of the Constitution does not change with the ebb and flow of economic events. We frequently are told in more general words that the Constitution must be construed in the light of the present. If by that it is meant that the Constitution is made up of living words that apply to every new condition which they include, the statement is quite true. But to say, if that be intended, that the words of the Constitution mean today what they did not mean when written—that is, that they do not apply to a situation now to which they would have applied then—is to rob that instrument of the essential element which continues it in force as the people have made it until they, and not their official agents, have made it otherwise. . . .

The judicial function is that of interpretation; it does not include the power of amendment under the guise of interpretation. To miss the point of difference between the two is to miss all that the phrase "supreme law of the land" stands for, and to convert what was intended as inescapable and enduring mandates into mere moral reflections. . . .

## The Soundness of *Adkins*

The *Adkins* case dealt with an act of Congress which had passed the scrutiny both of the legislative and executive branches of the government. We recognized that thereby these departments had affirmed the validity of the statute, and properly declared that their determination must be given great weight, but we then concluded, after thorough consideration, that their view could not be sustained. We think it not inappropriate now to add a word on that subject before coming to the question immediately under review.

The people, by their Constitution, created three separate, distinct, independent and coequal departments of government. The governmental structure rests, and was intended to rest, not upon any one or upon any two, but upon all three of these fundamental pillars. It seems unnecessary to repeat what so often has been said, that the powers of these departments are different, and are to be exercised independently. The differences clearly and definitely appear in the Constitution. Each of the departments is an agent of its creator, and one department is not and cannot be the agent of another. Each is answerable to its creator for what it does, and not to another agent. The view, therefore, of the Executive and of Congress that an act is constitutional is persuasive in a high degree; but it is not controlling.

Coming, then, to a consideration of the Washington statute, it first is to be observed that it is in every substantial respect identical with the statute involved in the *Adkins* case. Such vices as existed in the latter are present in the former. And if the *Adkins* case was properly decided, as we who join in this opinion think it was, it necessarily follows that the Washington statute is invalid.

In support of minimum wage legislation it has been urged, on the one hand, that great benefits will result in favor of underpaid labor, and, on the other hand, that the danger of such legislation is that the minimum will tend to become the maximum, and thus bring down the earnings of the more efficient toward the level of the less efficient employees. But with these speculations we have nothing to do. We are concerned only with the question of constitutionality.

That the clause of the Fourteenth Amendment which forbids a state to deprive any person of life, liberty or property without due process of law includes freedom of contract is so well settled as to be no longer open to question. Nor reasonably can it be disputed that contracts of employment of labor are included in the rule. . . .

In the *Adkins* case, we referred to this language, and said that, while there was no such thing as absolute freedom of contract, but that it was subject to a great variety of restraints, nevertheless, freedom of contract was the general rule, and restraint the exception, and that the power to abridge that freedom could only be justified by the existence of exceptional circumstances. This statement of the rule has been many times affirmed, and we do not understand that it is questioned by the present decision. . . .

## Fixing Wages for Women

We then pointed out that minimum wage legislation such as that here involved does not deal with any business charged with a public interest, or with public work, or with a temporary emergency, or with the character, methods or periods of wage payments, or with hours of labor, or with the protection of persons under legal disability, or with the prevention of fraud. It is, simply and exclusively, a law fixing wages for adult women who are legally as capable of contracting for themselves as men, and cannot be sustained unless upon principles apart from those involved in cases already decided by the court.

Two cases were involved in the *Adkins* decision. In one of them, it appeared that a woman 21 years of age, who brought the suit, was employed as an elevator operator at a fixed salary. Her services were satisfactory, and she was anxious to retain her position, and her employer, while willing to retain her, was obliged to dispense with her services on account of the penalties prescribed by the act. The wages received by her were the best she was able to obtain for any work she was capable of performing, and the enforcement of the order deprived her, as she alleged, not only of that employment, but left her unable to secure any position at which she could make a living with as good physical and moral surroundings and as good wages as she was receiving and was willing to take. The Washington statute, of course, admits of the same situation and result, and, for aught that appears to the contrary, the situation in the present case may have been the same as that just described. Certainly, to the extent that the statute applies to such cases, it cannot be justified as a reasonable restraint upon the freedom of contract. On the contrary, it is essentially arbitrary.

Neither the statute involved in the *Adkins* case nor the Washington statute, so far as it is involved here, has the slightest relation to the capacity or earning power of the employee, to the number of hours which constitute the day's work, the character of the place where the work is to be done, or the circumstances or surroundings of the employment. The sole basis upon which the question of validity rests is the assumption that the employee is entitled to receive a sum of money sufficient to provide a living for her, keep her in health, and preserve her morals. And, as we pointed out at some length in that case, the question thus presented for the determination of the board cannot be solved by any general formula prescribed by a statutory bureau, since it is not a composite, but an individual, question to be answered for each individual, considered by herself. . . .

## Women's Legal and Political Equality

The Washington statute, like the one for the District of Columbia, fixes minimum wages for adult women. Adult men and their employers are left free to bargain as they please, and it is a significant and an important fact that all state statutes to which our attention has been called are of like character. The common law rules restricting the power of women to make contracts have, under our system, long since practically disappeared. Women today stand upon a legal and political equality with men. There is no longer any reason why they should be put in different classes in respect of their legal right to make contracts; nor should they be denied, in effect, the right to compete with men for work paying lower wages which men may be willing to accept. And it is an arbitrary exercise of the legislative power to do so. . . .

An appeal to the principle that the legislature is free to recognize degrees of harm, and confine its restrictions accordingly, is but to beg the question, which is, since the contractual rights of men and women are the same, does the legislation here involved, by restricting only the rights of women to make contracts as to wages, create an arbitrary discrimination? We think it does. Difference of sex affords no reasonable ground for making a restriction applicable to the wage contracts of all working women from which like contracts of all working men are left free. Certainly a suggestion that the bargaining ability of the average woman is not equal to that of the average man would lack substance. The ability to make a fair bargain, as everyone knows, does not depend upon sex.

If, in the light of the facts, the state legislation, without reason or for reasons of mere expediency, excluded men from the provisions of the legislation, the power was exercised arbitrarily. On the other hand, if such legislation in respect of men was properly omitted on the ground that it would be unconstitutional, the same conclusion of unconstitutionality is inescapable in respect of similar legislative restraint in the case of women.

Finally, it may be said that a statute absolutely fixing wages in the various industries at definite sums and forbidding employers and employees from contracting for any other than those designated would probably not be thought to be constitutional. It is hard to see why the power to fix minimum wages does not connote a like power in respect of maximum wages. And yet, if both powers be exercised in such a way that the minimum and the maximum so nearly approach each other as to become substantially the same, the right to make any contract in respect of wages will have been completely abrogated.

*"The Court switched from invalidator to legitimator of the New Deal and . . . at the fulcrum were Justice Roberts and the minimum wage."*

# In Overturning *Adkins* the Supreme Court Switched from Opposing to Supporting the New Deal

*John W. Chambers*

*John W. Chambers taught history at California State College at Hayward (now California State University–East Bay). In his discussion of the minimum wage cases of the 1930s, he comments on the theory that Justice Owen Roberts, the Court's swing vote, changed his view of the constitutionality of the legislation for political expediency between the* Morehead v. New York ex rel. Tipaldo *case and* West Coast Hotel Co. v. Parrish. *In Tipaldo, Roberts had joined the conservative bloc of the bench and voted to strike down a New York minimum wage law for women and children. In* Parrish, *which involved a chambermaid suing her employer for back pay because what she had received was less than the Washington state minimum wage, Roberts voted to uphold the constitutionality of minimum wage legislation. Chambers concludes that President Franklin Delano Roosevelt's massive election victory of 1936 probably offers the best clue to*

John W. Chambers, "The Big Switch: Justice Roberts and the Minimum Wage Cases," *Labor History*, vol. 10, no. 1, 1969, pp. 58–66, 71–73. Copyright © 1969 Taylor & Francis Group, LLC. Reproduced by permission of Taylor & Francis, Ltd., http://www.tandf.co.uk/journals and the author.

*Roberts's change of position. After that point, he says, Roberts voted consistently to uphold the social and economic legislation of Roosevelt's New Deal.*

The Supreme Court hinted at judicial change [in a number of labor cases in the 1930s], but it was in another minimum-wage case that the Court demonstrated its dramatic shift in direction. On the same October [1936] day that it had denied the petition for rehearing in the *Tipaldo* [*Morehead v. New York ex rel. Tipaldo* (1936)] litigation, the Court—in a surprising move—had agreed to review a new minimum-wage case, *West Coast Hotel Co. v. Parrish*. The action originated in the State of Washington. Elsie Parrish, a former chambermaid at the Cascadian Hotel in Wenatchee, claimed that she had been paid less than the state minimum wage, and she demanded $216.19 in back pay. The local superior court had rejected her claim, but the Supreme Court of Washington State had upheld the constitutionality of the state's minimum-wage law, and had ordered that Mrs. Parrish be paid. The hotel owners had appealed to the Supreme Court of the United States.

## The Court Agrees to Hear the Case

The justices had considered the appeal between October 5 and 10. In conference, the question arose whether the Court should summarily reverse the Washington Supreme Court without explanation on the basis of the *Adkins* [*v. Children's Hospital* (1923)] and *Tipaldo* decisions. The four die-hard conservatives voted to do so. But [Justice Owen] Roberts later wrote that he had announced he would vote to hear the case. "I am not sure that I gave my reason," Roberts declared in 1945, "but it was that in the appeal in the *Parrish* case the authority of *Adkins* was definitely assailed and the Court was asked to reconsider and overrule it. Thus, for the first time, I was confronted with the necessity of facing the soundness of the *Ad-*

*kins* case." The conservatives expressed surprise, and one whispered to another, "What is the matter with Roberts?"

When the Court agreed to hear the *Parrish* case, many supporters of minimum-wage legislation were at first enthusiastic. But they quickly became pessimistic. They believed that if the Court had refused to hear the appeal, the Washington law would have continued to operate, but by hearing the case, the Court would have a chance to terminate the law. There was soon almost unanimous agreement in the nation's capital that the Supreme Court would eventually invalidate the Washington State minimum-wage law as unconstitutional.

Arguments in the *Parrish* case were heard by the Supreme Court on December 16 and 17, a little more than one month after the presidential election. [Harlan] Stone was still convalescing at home and did not hear the case. Counsel for the hotel company challenged the law as a violation of freedom of contract. He charged that the 1913 Washington state minimum-wage law was identical with the District of Columbia statute invalidated in the *Adkins* decision. Indeed, the two laws were virtually the same. They were both primarily concerned with fixing a wage high enough to maintain working women in good health. There was no attempt to relate wages to the work performed, as New York had tried to do. The hotel company's lawyer claimed the *Adkins* and *Tipaldo* precedents showed clearly that minimum-wage legislation was unconstitutional. Mrs. Parrish's attorneys, on the other hand, held that the Constitution permitted reasonable regulation for the public welfare and that the statute was within the police power of the state when fixing a minimum wage for women hotel employees.

## Finding in Favor of the Minimum Wage

In a private talk with [chief justice Charles] Hughes, apparently after the arguments, Roberts said he would vote to uphold the Washington state minimum-wage law. Hughes was so happy that he felt like hugging the burly Roberts. Two days after the oral arguments were completed, the justices discussed the *Parrish* case at their weekly conference. Stone was still absent. Since the justices vote in reverse order of seniority—the most recent member first—[Benjamin] Cardozo cast the first vote. He voted to affirm. Roberts was next. He cast his crucial ballot in favor of minimum-wage legislation. The decision had been made; the others voted quickly: [Pierce] Butler against, [George] Sutherland against, [Louis] Brandeis for, [James] McReynolds against, [Willis] Van Devanter against, and Chief Justice Hughes in favor. The Court was split four-to-four, which meant that the decision of the Washington Supreme Court would stand, and the statute would be upheld. But Chief Justice Hughes wanted to avoid such a weak affirmation of minimum-wage legislation. Since the justices knew that Stone would vote in favor of the law and provide a five-to-four majority on such an important issue, they agreed to hold the case over until the ailing jurist returned.

Stone convalesced until about February 1 when he rejoined the Court. Within the next few days, the *Parrish* case was once again brought up at the judges' conference, and Stone voted in favor of upholding the minimum-wage law. The vote was now five-to-four, and the Chief Justice assigned the writing of the majority opinion to himself.

On February 5, 1937, President [Franklin Delano] Roosevelt startled the Court and the country by announcing his plan to reorganize the federal judiciary. The plan, which would enable the President to appoint up to six new Supreme Court justices as well as forty-four new judges to the other federal courts, was quickly dubbed an attempt to "pack the Supreme Court." Hughes delayed announcing the *Parrish* decision for nearly two months so that it would not appear as if the Court had reversed its position on minimum-wage legislation as a direct response to the President's court plan.

The Supreme Court building was packed with spectators on Monday, March 29, 1937. Throngs of Easter visitors had invaded the lofty marble-walled courtroom, and a line of sightseers curved down the long hallway. The Chief Justice read his majority opinion in the *Parrish* case to a packed house. Abandoning his compromise position in the *Tipaldo* case, he now accepted the strong pronouncements of Stone's dissent. First, he disposed of the *Tipaldo* case by saying that the majority had invalidated the New York law because it thought the statute was essentially the same as the District of Columbia law and because New York had not asked the Court to reconsider the *Adkins* decision. But Hughes declared that since the Washington Supreme Court had refused to regard *Adkins* as controlling, the 1923 precedent was now directly challenged. Second, in a lightning blow, Hughes overturned the *Adkins* precedent entirely and terminated the thirty-year-old doctrine of freedom of contract. "What is this freedom?" Hughes asked. "The Constitution does not speak of freedom of contract. It speaks of liberty and prohibits the deprivation of liberty without due process of law. . . . Liberty under the Constitution is thus necessarily subject to the restraints of due process, and regulation which is reasonable in relation to its subject and is adopted in the interests of the community is due process." Hughes cited many previous decisions to show that contracts between employer and employee could be restricted in the public interest. The doctrine of freedom of contract was dead.

## Sutherland's Dissent

Justice Sutherland, the leader of the reactionary bloc who was appointed to the Court by Harding in 1922, wrote the dissent for his fellow conservatives in what his biographer claims was clearly a defense of his entire judicial career. He declared that the Constitution had given the Court the role of preventing the power which that document segregated into different branches and divisions of government from coming together to threaten the liberty of the individual. The function of the Supreme Court, Sutherland warned the new majority, "does not include the power of amendment under the guise of interpretation.... If the Constitution ... stands in the way of desirable legislation, the blame must rest upon that instrument and not upon the court for enforcing it according to its terms. The remedy in that situation—and the only true remedy—is to amend the Constitution." It was an eloquent statement of the concept of a judge as an impartial instrument determining whether contested statutes squared with the Constitution, but the new concept of legal realism with its recognition of the personal biases of judges made it as obsolete as unlimited freedom of contract in an age of giant corporations.

## Roberts' Switch

Newspaper headlines told the story. "MINIMUM WAGE LAW CONSTITUTIONAL; SUPREME COURT SWITCH DUE TO ROBERTS," announced *The New York Times*. In the Senate chamber, Democratic majority leader Joseph Robinson broke into the debate over the court plan to tell the news in his Arkansas drawl. Swinging both fists over his head to drive home his point, he yelled: "I would like to refer to the fact that the Supreme Court has reversed itself in the Adkins case and probably in the New York Wage Case." The ruling had a decisive impact on the general public. Public opinion polls showed that, following the decision, the number of Americans favoring the President's court plan began a decline from which it never recovered. Roosevelt, however, was not convinced. He thought the switch only indicated how the legality of legislation could be determined by the whim of one justice. There was nothing to prevent Roberts from switching back again. Even weeks later, Roosevelt believed that the Court-imposed "no-man's land" of 1936 had only been replaced by a "Roberts' Land."

"White Monday," March 29, 1937, was the Supreme Court's day of atonement. Not only did the Court uphold minimum-wage legislation that day, but it also sanctioned legislation promoting collective bargaining for railroad workers, providing relief for bankrupt farmers, and using the taxing power to control interstate shipments of pistols and rifles. "What a day!" recalled Assistant Attorney General Robert H. Jackson a few years later. "The Court was on the march!" After *Parrish* came the deluge. Fourteen days later, the Court upheld the National Labor Relations Act by brushing aside its own edicts in the *AAA* and *Carter Coal* decisions and accepting an expanded definition of interstate commerce which would allow Congress to regulate industrial and labor relations. Two months after White Monday, the Court upheld the Social Security Act by agreeing to both an employer tax and conditional federal grants-in-aid. In 1941, the Supreme Court's attitude toward social and economic legislation was so changed from the days of the *Adkins* and *Tipaldo* decisions that the justices unanimously upheld minimum-wage regulations at rates above the subsistence level for men as well as women.

After thirty years, the road was clear for minimum-wage legislation. The United States began to catch up to the rest of the modern world in protecting its workers against starvation wages. A jubilant Mary Dewson, one of the directors of the National Consumers' League, beamed with joy. "Isn't everything today exciting?" she wrote two weeks after the *Parrish* ruling. "Just to think that silly Roberts should have the power to play politics and decide the fate of Minimum-Wage legislation. But, thank God he thought it was politically expedient to be with us!"

Did Roberts really switch between the *Tipaldo* and *Parrish* decisions as so many contemporaries believed? And if so, why? Most of Roberts' correspondence apparently was destroyed, but a memorandum written by him nearly ten years later denies that he had changed between the two cases. In it, Roberts supported Hughes' argument in the *Parrish* opinion that the Court had not switched at all because it had not been confronted with a direct challenge to *Adkins* until the *Parrish* case. Felix Frankfurter, the Harvard law professor and unofficial adviser to Roosevelt, was convinced in 1937 that Roberts had switched for political reasons. But later, when he and Roberts sat together on the Supreme Court, Frankfurter changed his opinion. Both Frankfurter and Dean Erwin Griswold of the Harvard Law School have insisted that Roberts did not switch at all. They pictured Roberts as a conscientious legal craftsman truly concerned with the details of the law and neglectful of popular reaction and his own reputation. According to the Roberts-Frankfurter-Griswold argument, Roberts apparently wanted to overrule *Adkins* and uphold minimum-wage legislation all along, but he was prohibited in the Spring of 1936 by a technicality, the timid and disingenuous arguments of the attorneys for the state of New York.

In reality, Roberts appears to have switched both in mind and in vote. His vote invalidated minimum-wage legislation in the *Tipaldo* case and upheld it in the *Parrish* case. His actions tell more about his attitude than do his later recollections. His 1945 argument about technicalities and timidity in the New York case seems more like sophistry than excess legal craftsmanship. The fact is that Roberts could have upheld the New York minimum-wage law—and thus minimum-wage legislation in general—if he had wanted to do so. There were alternatives.

New York's counsel had offered the Court an escape-hatch through which it could uphold the depression-spawned minimum-wage law while at the same time preserving *Adkins* and presumably the prestige and stability of the Court's line of reasoning. Hughes saw this and took it; Roberts refused.

There were actual differences between the New York and the District of Columbia statutes. They were there if Roberts had wanted to recognize them. Two top legal craftsmen, Frankfurter and [Benjamin] Cohen, had drafted a minimum-wage bill designed to avoid the legal pitfalls expressed in the *Adkins* opinion. Admittedly, the statutes were basically the same in their aim, and the differences were minor, but the variations were no more technical than the point on which Roberts based his stand in the *Tipaldo* decision. They were sufficient for Hughes in his dissenting opinion. The majority's argument that it was bound by the New York Court of Appeals' construction of the law and could not assess the intent of the lawmakers was an attempt to avoid considering the statute on its merits. It is debatable whether a construction of a law by a state's highest court was binding on the Supreme Court. . . .

While there is no explicit answer to why Roberts changed his mind, the events of 1936–37 offer an excellent clue. The timing of Roberts' shift in attitude toward minimum wages and the New Deal indicates that the main reason was probably Roosevelt's massive election victory in November 1936.

Despite Roberts' attempt to prove otherwise, his switch apparently came after the election. Roberts' claim in his 1945 memorandum that he voted about Oct. 10, 1936 to hear the *Parrish* case is *not* conclusive evidence that he had decided to support minimum-wage legislation. The actual vote was not recorded, and since only four votes were needed to grant probable jurisdiction, it could have been granted whether Roberts voted with Hughes and the liberals or not. Even if Roberts did vote to hear the case, it did not mean that he intended to vote in favor of the Washington State minimum-wage law. Once again his memo is ambiguous. "I am not sure that I gave my reason," he wrote, "but it was that in the appeal in the *Parrish* case the authority of *Adkins* was definitely assailed and the Court was asked to reconsider and overrule it. Thus, for the first time, I was confronted with the necessity of facing the soundness of the *Adkins* case." Roberts did not say he was ready to overrule *Adkins*, and he could have been merely postponing action (the arch-conservative wanted to invalidate the law summarily) until after the November election in order to get a clearer picture of the public's reaction to the New Deal and to gauge the danger to the Court. Further, Hughes' biographical notes seem to indicate that he was not aware that Roberts was ready to uphold minimum-wage legislation until after the oral arguments in *Parrish* in December.

The first verified evidence of Roberts' switch came after the election. Within two or three weeks after the Roosevelt landslide, Roberts ended his year-and-a-half alliance with the conservatives and voted with the liberals to uphold the New York Unemployment Insurance Act. And at the weekly conference on December 19, 1936, according to written recollections by both Hughes and Roberts, he voted to uphold minimum-wage legislation in the *Parrish* case.

Mr. Dooley, the philosophical Irish bartender created by columnist Finley Peter Dunne, once commented on the Supreme Court's 1901 decision in the Insular Cases regarding American citizenship in the territories. His conclusion became immortal.

"But there's wan thing I'm sure about."

"What's that?" asked Mr. Hennessy.

"That is," said Mr. Dooley, "no matter whether th' constitution follows th' flag or not, th' supreme court follows th' iliction returns."

Once again the Supreme Court had followed the election returns. The size of the Roosevelt victory reinforced the criticism which had been directed against the Court for its 1935—36 epic-sized binge against social and economic legislation. It seemed to reach a crescendo in the protest against the *Tipaldo* ruling, one of the most criticized decisions in Supreme Court history. The public seemed almost unanimously opposed to the sweeping invalidation of state minimum-wage legislation for women and children. In effect, the people, through their reaction to the decision, legitimized minimum-wage regulation as a reasonable use of the state's police powers.

After voting with the conservatives from May 1935 to October 1936, Roberts joined the liberals in November 1936 to uphold the New York Unemployment Insurance Act, and the next month to sustain minimum-wage legislation. Throughout the Court's 1936—37 term, he voted consistently with the liberals to uphold the social and economic legislation of the New Deal. The President's court-plan, coming after the switch had begun, probably reinforced Roberts' and Hughes' awareness that the Court was in jeopardy if it did not yield. In 1954, Roberts admitted that he had been "fully conscious of the tremendous strain and threat to the existing Court" inherent in the reorganization plan.

Thus a combination of pressures—presidential, congressional, and most important, public—convinced Roberts that he must accept the new philosophy and interpret the Constitution in line with the times. In the expression of the day, "a switch in time saved nine." The Court switched from invalidator to legitimator of the New Deal and emerged unscathed. It was perhaps the greatest switch in the Court's history, and at the fulcrum were Justice Roberts and the minimum wage.

> *"Once Roosevelt had a 5-4 majority for [his] social legislation, there no longer appeared to be an urgent need for a [Court-packing plan]."*

# *Parrish*'s Support of New Deal Policies Obviated FDR's "Court-Packing" Plan

*William E. Leuchtenburg*

*William E. Leuchtenburg is the William Rand Kenan Jr. Professor of History emeritus at the University of North Carolina at Chapel Hill. In the following viewpoint, he describes the* West Coast Hotel Co. v. Parrish *decision and how it bolstered public support for President Franklin Roosevelt's New Deal policies. In the case, Elsie Parrish, a hotel chambermaid, sued her employer for back wages, claiming she was due the difference between what she had been paid and what she would have received had she been paid Washington state's minimum wage. After the defeat of minimum wage legislation in* Adkins v. Children's Hospital *thirteen years earlier, it was assumed that things would not go her way. However, the Supreme Court, in a stunning reversal, found for Parrish. Leuchtenburg describes the high drama in the Court that day, noting how chief justice Charles Evans Hughes presented his opinion with confidence, despite widespread criticism that he was bowing to pressure from outside forces. After a string of legislative defeats, President Roosevelt had suggested that he would use his powers to "reform" the judiciary—which according to many meant "packing" the Court with justices sym-*

William E. Leuchtenburg, "The Case of the Chambermaid and the Nine Old Men," *American Heritage*, vol. 38, December 1986, pp. 34–41. Copyright © 1986 American Heritage. A Division of Forbes, Inc. Reproduced by permission of the author.

*pathetic to his economic policies. When the* Parrish *decision reversed* Adkins, *many conservatives felt that the justices were trampling on the Constitution because of political pressure—and that the decision had been made to protect the Court. Leuchtenburg explains the dismayed reaction to* Parrish *among conservatives who were opposed to the minimum wage and the boost in support accorded the president and his policies after the decision.*

When, on a spring day in 1935, Elsie Parrish walked into the office of an obscure lawyer in Wenatchee, Washington, to ask him to sue the town's leading hotel for back pay, she had no idea she was linking her fate to that of exploited women in a Brooklyn laundry a whole continent away. Still less did she think that she was setting off a series of events that would deeply affect President Franklin D. Roosevelt's plans for his second term. Least of all did she perceive that she was triggering a constitutional revolution that, even today, remains the most significant chapter in the two centuries of existence of the United States Supreme Court. All that Elsie knew was that she had been bilked.

Late in the summer of 1933, Elsie Lee, a woman of about forty who would soon be Elsie Parrish, had taken a job as a chambermaid at the Cascadian Hotel in Wenatchee, entrepôt [a trade hub] for a beautiful recreation area reaching from the Columbia valley to the Cascades, and the country's foremost apple market. . . . Elsie worked irregularly over the next year and a half at cleaning toilets and sweeping rugs for an hourly wage of twenty-two cents, later raised to a quarter. When she was discharged in May 1935, she asked for back pay of $216.19, the difference between what she had received and what she would have gotten if she had been paid each week the $14.50 minimum wage required for her occupation under state law. The Cascadian, which was owned by the West Coast Hotel Company, offered to settle for a total of $17.00, but she would not hear of it. Instead, she, together with her husband, Ernest, brought suit for all that was due her.

## Washington's Minimum Wage Law

Elsie and Ernest rested their case on the provisions of a statute that had been enacted by Washington State a quarter of a century before when, catching the contagion of reform from neighboring Oregon, the state legislature had taken steps to wipe out sweatshops. The 1913 act declared it "unlawful to employ women or minors . . . under conditions of labor detrimental to their health or morals; and . . . to employ women workers in any industry . . . at wages which are not adequate for their maintenance." To safeguard the welfare of female employees, the law established a commission that was authorized to call together employers, employees, and representatives of the public who would recommend a wage standard "not detrimental to health and morals, and which shall be sufficient for the decent maintenance of women." On receiving that recommendation, the commission was to issue an order stipulating the minimum wage that must be paid. For chambermaids, the weekly minimum was set at $14.50. Twice the statute had been challenged in the courts, and on both occasions the Washington Supreme Court had validated the act. Elsie Parrish appeared to have an airtight case.

Alas, any law student in the land could have told her that her case was hopeless, for, twelve years before, the United States Supreme Court had ruled, in a widely reported decision, *Adkins v. Children's Hospital*, that a minimum wage act for women was unconstitutional because it violated the liberty of contract that the Court claimed was guaranteed by the Constitution. Though the opinion by Justice George Sutherland commanded only five votes and elicited vigorous dissents, it reconfirmed a notion incorporated in constitutional doctrine only a generation before: that a great corporation and its employee—even someone as powerless as a chambermaid—each has an equivalent right to bargain about wages, a fantasy that Justice Oliver Wendell Holmes dismissed as "dogma" and the renowned commentator Thomas Reed Powell of Harvard Law School called "indefensible."*Adkins*, said one commentator, "makes forever impossible all other legislation along similar lines involving the regulation of wages." In principle Elsie's case was no different from *Adkins*. Any statute that deprived a person of life, liberty, or property, without due process of law, was disallowed. Though the Washington law remained on the books, it was presumed to be null and void. Hence, it startled no one when, in November 1935, after hearing Elsie's case, the presiding judge of the Superior Court of Chelan County, explaining that *Adkins* bound every court in the nation, ruled against her.

Surprisingly, the Supreme Court of the state of Washington took a different view. On April 2, 1936, it overturned the lower court's decision, thereby finding in Elsie Parrish's favor. To get around the huge obstacle of *Adkins*, the court pointed out that the U.S. Supreme Court had never struck down a *state* minimum wage law, which was true but irrelevant. The decision gave the Parrishes a moment of euphoria, but it hardly seemed likely that this opinion would, in the light of *Adkins* and the hostility of Justices such as Sutherland, survive a test in the United States Supreme Court.

## The *Tipaldo* Case

Just eight weeks later the U.S. Supreme Court settled any doubt on that matter by a decision on a case that, three thousand miles from Wenatchee, had begun to wend its way through the judicial system while Elsie Parrish was still making beds in the Cascadian Hotel. It arose out of the hope of social reformers in New York, especially women active in the Consumers' League, that the Court, despite *Adkins*, might look favorably on a minimum wage law for women and minors if it was drafted to emphasize the value of the services rendered as well as the needs of women. To that end Felix Frankfurter of Harvard Law School and Benjamin Cohen, a former law clerk of Justice [Louis] Brandeis, crafted a model law. New

York State adopted it in 1933, during the fourth year of a great depression that had reduced some young women, paid starvation wages, to sleeping on subways. Frankfurter warned that it was "foolish beyond words" to expect the Court to reverse itself, but he hoped that the Justices might be willing to distinguish this statute, with its added feature of "value of services," from the one struck down in *Adkins.* "Every word" of the New York law, explained a prominent woman reformer, was "written with the Supreme Court of the United States in mind."

In accordance with the provisions of the model legislation, New York State obtained an indictment against Joseph Tipaldo, manager of the Spotlight Laundry in Brooklyn, who had been brutally exploiting his nine female employees, first by paying them far below the state minimum wage and then by pretending to pay the minimum but forcing the sweatshop laundresses to kick back the difference between what the state required and what he actually intended to pay. When Joe Tipaldo went to jail to stand trial on charges of disobeying the mandatory wage order and of forgery, the hotel industry (the same business that would be involved in the *Parrish* case) rushed to his side with an offer to bankroll a test of the constitutionality of the New York law. Since hotels were working their employees twelve hours a day, seven days a week, they had a high stake in the case. In fact, the state had already begun minimum wage proceedings against them. Consequently, each hotel put money in a kitty to finance Tipaldo's petition for a writ of habeas corpus to compel the warden of Brooklyn's city prison to release the laundry manager from custody. While his case was being prepared, Tipaldo, utterly shameless, renamed his firm the Bright Light Laundry and made a big investment in expanding his business. He explained, "I expect to get it back eventually on what I save in wages."

On June 1, 1936, the United States Supreme Court appeared to justify his optimism when, in a 5-4 decision, it struck down New York's minimum wage law. In a sweeping opinion by one of the most conservative Justices, the Court said that there was no meaningful difference between the New York statute and the D.C. act that had been invalidated in *Adkins*, for both violated the liberty of contract that safeguarded equally the rights of employer and employee to bargain about wages. After quoting from *Adkins* with obvious approval, the Court declared, in language that shocked champions of social reform, "The decision and the reasoning upon which it rests clearly show that the State is without power by any form of legislation to prohibit, change or nullify contracts between employers and adult women workers as to the amount of wages to be paid." Those words all but doomed Elsie Parrish's cause, and gave Joe Tipaldo the victory of a lifetime.

That victory, however, turned out to carry a very high price. "After the court decision, business looked good for a while," Joe told a reporter three months later. "I was able to undercharge my competitors a little on what I saved in labor costs." But then business started to fall off, then fell some more. "I think this fight was the cause of my trouble," he said. "My customers wouldn't give my drivers their wash." Before the summer was over, the Bright Light Laundry had folded and Joe Tipaldo was unemployed. "I'm broke now," he confessed. "I couldn't stand the gaff [ordeal]."

The *Tipaldo* decision, though, engendered a powerful backlash, not least from some of the members of the Supreme Court. In a strongly worded dissent, Chief Justice Charles Evans Hughes upbraided the majority for failing to acknowledge either that the New York law differed from the statute in *Adkins* or that the state has "the power to protect women from being exploited by overreaching employers. . . ." Far more biting was the separate dissent filed by Justice Harlan Fiske Stone on behalf of himself and his fellow Justices Louis Brandeis and Benjamin Cardozo. In one of the most scathing criticisms ever uttered from the bench, Stone accused the

Court of indulging its "own personal economic predilections," for he found "grim irony in speaking of the freedom of contract of those who, because of their economic necessities, give their services for less than is needful to keep body and soul together." In an impassioned warning to his brethren to exercise more self-restraint, Stone asserted, "The Fourteenth Amendment has no more embedded in the Constitution our preference for some particular set of economic beliefs than it has adopted, in the name of liberty, the system of theology which we may happen to approve."

Much of the nation shared Stone's sense of indignation about *Tipaldo*. Secretary of the Interior Harold Ickes noted angrily in his diary: "The sacred right of liberty of contract again—the right of an immature child or a helpless woman to drive a bargain with a great corporation. If this decision does not outrage the moral sense of the country, then nothing will." A Republican newspaper in upstate New York declared, "The law that would jail any laundry-man for having an underfed horse should jail him for having an underfed girl employee."

## No "Special Privileges" for Women

Only two groups applauded the decision. One was the press in a scattering of cheap-labor towns undismayed by the fact that, following the ruling, the wages of laundresses—mostly impoverished blacks and Puerto Rican and Italian migrants—were slashed in half. The other was a small faction of advanced feminists centered in Alice Paul's National Woman's Party.... Their argument was that there should be no special privileges for women—that putting them in a protected category was discriminatory and demeaning. Most women activists, though, were horrified by that view, which they believed reflected the dogmatism of upper-class ladies who had no familiarity with the suffering of workers. They were as devoted as Alice Paul to equal rights, and they must have shuddered at the paternalism implicit in earlier opinions sustaining separate treatment for women on the grounds that they were wards of the state. But they were sure that female employees required protection, and they knew that insistence on the principle of equal rights meant no minimum wage law whatsoever, since the Court, as constituted in FDR's first term, would never sanction social legislation for men. "Thus," the historian Mary Beard wrote Justice Stone, Alice Paul "plays into the hands of the rawest capitalists." . . .

*Tipaldo*, handed down on the final day of the term, climaxed an extraordinary thirteen months in which the Court struck down more important socioeconomic legislation than at any time in history. During that brief period it destroyed the two foundation stones of Roosevelt's recovery program, the National Industrial Recovery Act [NIRA] and the Agricultural Adjustment Act; turned thumbs down on a number of other New Deal laws and state reforms; and cavalierly rebuked the President and his appointees. The NIRA ruling had been unanimous, but almost all the others had come in split decisions, most often with the "Four Horsemen," Pierce Butler, James McReynolds, George Sutherland, and Willis Van Devanter, a quartet of adamantly conservative judges, joined in the spring of 1935 by the youngest member of the bench, Owen Roberts. . . .

## FDR's "Court-Packing Plan"

Despite the enormous setbacks the New Deal had sustained, Franklin Roosevelt gave every indication that he was accepting his losses virtually without complaint. . . . While Elsie Parrish's feeble case was advancing toward its final reckoning in the United States Supreme Court, the President gave not the slightest indication that he had any plans whatsoever to make the Justices any less refractory, for it seemed to him altogether inadvisable in the 1936 presidential campaign to hand his opponents, who were hard put to find an issue, an opportunity to stand by the Constitution. As late as the end of January 1937, after FDR had delivered his State of the Union message and his Inaugural address, the editor of *United States Law Week* wrote that "last week it was made plain that he does not at the present time have in mind any legislation directed at the Court."

Less than two weeks later, on February 5, 1937, the President stunned the country by sending a special message to Congress that constituted the boldest attempt a Chief Executive has ever initiated to remold the judiciary. He recommended that when a federal judge who had served at least ten years waited more than six months after his seventieth birthday to resign or retire, the President could add a new judge to the bench. Since this was the most aged Court in history—they were referred to as the "nine old men"—Roosevelt would be able to add as many as six new Supreme Court Justices. He claimed he was presenting this proposal as a way of expediting litigation, but it was widely understood that what he really wanted was a more amenable tribunal. From the very first day, his program was saddled with a designation it could never shake off: the "Court-packing plan."

Though FDR's scheme provoked fierce protests, political analysts anticipated that it would be adopted. By winning in a landslide in 1936, Roosevelt had carried so many members of his party into Congress that the Republicans were left with only sixteen of the ninety-six seats in the Senate and fewer than one hundred of the more than four hundred seats in the House. So long as the Court continued to strike down New Deal reforms—and such vital legislation as the Social Security Act was still to be decided on—it was highly unlikely that enough Democrats would desert their immensely popular President to defeat the measure. The very first evidence of the attitude of the Court would come with its decision on Elsie Parrish's case, and there was every expectation that, acting not many months after *Tipaldo*, the Court would render an adverse ruling that would improve Roosevelt's already excellent chances. On the very day the *Parrish* decision was to be handed down, March 29, 1937, the president of the National Women's Republican Club declared, "I don't see how the President's bill can fail to get a majority." . . .

## The *Parrish* Decision

The unusually protracted time of 103 days had elapsed since Elsie Parrish's case had been argued, and it was to be the first judgment handed down since FDR had suggested packing the Court. Some twelve thousand visitors flocked to the building in anticipation that this would be journey's end for the suit that had begun nearly two years earlier. . . .

The Chief Justice leaned forward in his chair, picked up some sheets of paper, and announced, "This case presents the question of the constitutional validity of the minimum wage law of the State of Washington." . . . Hughes, fully aware of the effect he was having and surely conscious of his magnificent appearance (with his patrician features, sparkling eyes, and well-groomed beard, he was often likened to [the Roman god] Jove), raised his voice to overcome the bustle, then paused and peered out over the crowded chamber for a moment before returning to his written opinion.

Not for some time did Hughes indicate what the Court had decided. Anxious minutes passed as he labored through a reprise of the facts in the case, and when he finally took up one of the arguments of Elsie Parrish's attorneys, he did so only to reject it disdainfully. It was "obviously futile," he said, for counsel to claim that present case could be distinguished from *Adkins* on the grounds that Mrs. Parrish had worked for a "hotel and that the business of an innkeeper was affected with a public interest." As it happened, he noted, one of the cases *Adkins* had disposed of had dealt with a hotel employee. If the Washington State law was to survive the day, it would need a better justification than this rickety effort.

It took only a moment more for Hughes to reveal that the Court was prepared to meet *Adkins* head on. Unlike *Tipaldo*, where the U.S. Supreme Court had felt bound by the ruling of the Court of Appeals of New York that the New York minimum wage act could not be distinguished from the statute in *Adkins* and hence was invalid, *Parrish*, the Chief Justice declared, presented a quite different situation, for the highest tribunal of the state of Washington had refused to be guided by *Adkins* and had sanctioned the law in dispute. . . . Careful examination of the doctrine of freedom of contract that had bulked so large in *Adkins* [was in order].

"What is this freedom?" Hughes inquired, his voice rising. "The Constitution does not speak of freedom of contract." Instead, the Constitution spoke of liberty and forbade denial of liberty without due process of law. The Constitution did not recognize absolute liberty, however. "The liberty safeguarded is liberty in a social organization," he declared. "Liberty under the Constitution is thus necessarily subject to the restraints of due process, and regulation which is reasonable in relation to its subject and is adopted in the interests of the community is due process." . . .

The Court had long since established that the State had especial authority to circumscribe the freedom of contract of women, the Chief Justice continued. In *Muller v. Oregon* (1908), he pointed out, the Court had fully elaborated the reasons for accepting a special sphere of State regulation of female labor in that landmark case the Court had emphasized, in the words of Justice David Brewer, that because a woman performs "maternal functions" her health "becomes an object of public interest and care in order to preserve the strength and vigor of the race." Hence, Brewer had gone on, a woman was "properly placed in a class by herself, and legislation designed for her protection may be sustained even when like legislation is not necessary for men and could not be sustained." The State could restrict her freedom of contract, the Court had determined, not merely "for her benefit, but also largely for the benefit of all."

The precedents established by *Muller* and several later rulings had led the dissenters in *Adkins* to believe that the D.C. minimum wage law should have been sustained, and with good reason, Hughes asserted. The dissenting Justices had challenged the distinction the majority in *Adkins* had drawn between maximum hours legislation (valid) and minimum wage statutes (invalid), and that challenge remained "without any satisfactory answer." The Washington State law was essentially the same as the D.C. act that had been struck down in *Adkins*, he acknowledged, "but we are unable to conclude that in its minimum wage requirement the State has passed beyond the boundary of its broad protective power." In that sentence, however convoluted, Hughes had said what for some minutes past it had been clear he was going to say: the Supreme Court was sustaining Washington's minimum wage law. Against all odds, Elsie Parrish had won. . . .

*Adkins*, written by Sutherland and carrying the votes of a number of Hughes's other brethren, was being put to death in its fifteenth year. One could not possibly reconcile *Adkins*, Hughes maintained, with "well-considered" rulings such as *Muller*. "What can be closer to the public interest than the health of women and their protection from unscrupulous and overreaching employers?" he asked. "And if the protection of women is a legitimate end of the exercise of state power, how can it be said that the requirement of the payment of a minimum wage fairly fixed in order to meet the very necessities of existence is not an admissible means to that end?"

With an eloquence, even passion, few thought him capable of, the Chief Justice added: "The legislature of the State was clearly entitled to consider the situation of women in employment, the fact that they are in the class receiving the least pay, that their bargaining power is relatively weak, and that they are the ready victims of those who would take advantage of their necessitous circumstances. The legislature was entitled to adopt measures to reduce the evils of the 'sweating system,' the exploiting of workers at wages so low as to be insufficient to meet the bare cost of living, thus making their very helplessness the occasion of a most injurious competition."

Since many states had adopted laws of this nature to remedy the evil of sweatshop competition, the enactment of such legislation by the state of Washington could not be viewed as "arbitrary or capricious, and that is all we have to decide," Hughes said. "Even if the wisdom of the policy be regarded as debatable and its effects uncertain, still the legislature is entitled to its judgment." Delighted at what they were hearing, the New Deal lawyers in the chamber smiled broadly and nudged one another.

## Exploitation Burdens the Community

In his closing remarks the Chief Justice advanced an "additional and compelling" reason for sustaining the statute. The exploitation of "relatively defence-less" employees not only injured those women, he asserted, but directly burdened the community, because "what these workers lose in wages the taxpayers are called upon to pay." With respect to that reality, he said, the Court took "judicial notice of the unparalleled demands" the Great Depression had made upon localities.... "The community is not bound to provide what is in effect a subsidy for unconscionable employers. The community may direct its law-making power to correct the abuse which springs from their selfish disregard of the public interest." Consequently, the Chief Justice concluded, "The case of *Adkins v. Children's Hospital* ... should be, and it is, overruled," and the judgment of the Supreme Court of the state of Washington on behalf of Elsie Parrish "is affirmed." Some two years after she changed sheets in the Cascadian Hotel for the last time, the Wenatchee chambermaid was to receive her $216.19 in back pay.

It would require some time for Court watchers to grasp the full implications of Hughes's opinion in *Parrish*—to write of the "Constitutional Revolution of 1937"—but George Sutherland's dissent revealed that the Four Horsemen understood at that very moment that their long reign, going all the way back to *Adkins* and even before, with only slight interruption, had abruptly ended. When, having spoken the final words, the Chief Justice nodded to Justice Sutherland seated to his left, Sutherland surveyed the chamber silently, almost diffidently, before picking up the sheaf of papers in front of him and beginning to read. Sensing his day had passed, Sutherland appeared barely able to bring himself to carry out his futile assignment. He started off speaking in a curiously toneless murmur, and even those nearby had trouble at first catching his words. In the rear of the room, all was lost.

## Sutherland's Dissent

Consequently, not a few missed altogether Sutherland's first sentence, and even those who did hear it needed a moment to take in its full import. . . .

After no more than a cursory paragraph saying that all the contentions that had just been advanced in *Parrish* had been adequately disposed of in *Adkins* and *Tipaldo*, Sutherland delivered a dissent that for quite some time constituted less a reply to Hughes and the majority in *Parrish* than to Justice Stone's 1936 calls for judicial restraint in cases such as *Tipaldo*. . . .

The elderly judge . . . went so far as to rap his knuckles on the dais as he took issue with the President, though never by name; with Justice Roberts, no longer his ally; and even more vigorously, again without mentioning him directly, with Justice Stone. In rebuttal to the Chief Justice's assertion that the case before the Court required a fresh examination, in part because of the "economic conditions which have supervened,"

Sutherland stated bluntly, "The meaning of the Constitution does not change with the ebb and flow of economic events."

When, having read nearly five pages of his opinion, Sutherland finally turned to the case before the Court, he said little more than that *West Coast Hotel Co.* replicated the situation in *Adkins*. In every important regard, the two statutes involved had identical "vices," Sutherland maintained, "and if the *Adkins* case was properly decided, as we who join in this opinion think it was, it necessarily follows that the Washington statute is invalid." It was beyond dispute, he asserted, that the due process clause embraced freedom of contract, and Sutherland remained convinced, too, that women stood on an equal plane with men and that legislation denying them the right to contract for low-paying jobs was discriminatory. . . .

When news of the momentous decision, relayed swiftly to every part of the nation over press association wires, reached Sutherland's supporters, they shared his sense of dismay. Conservatives were outraged. If FDR wanted a political court, said a disgruntled senator, he had one now, for the decision was blatantly political, a transparent effort to kill the Court-packing bill by demonstrating that the judges would no longer misbehave. Ardent feminists were no less incensed. One of them wrote Sutherland: "May I say that the minority opinion handed down in the Washington minimum wage case is, to me, what the rainbow was to Mr. Wordsworth? . . . You did my sex the honor of regarding women as persons and citizens."

## Mixed Reactions

Most reformers, though, women as well as men, hailed the *Parrish* ruling as a triumph for social justice and a vindication for FDR, who had been accorded an altogether unexpected victory in the most improbable quarter. One outspoken progressive, the columnist Heywood Broun, commented: "Mr. Roosevelt has been effective not only in forcing a major switch in judicial policy, but he has even imposed something of his style upon the majority voice of the court. There are whole sections in the document written and read by Chief Justice Hughes which sound as if they might have been snatched bodily from [the weekly FDR radio address to the American people known as a] fireside chat."

Partisans of the President jeered at the Court for its abrupt reversal of views on the validity of minimum wage legislation. Because of the "change of a judicial mind," observed the attorney general, Homer Cummings, sardonically, "the Constitution on Monday, March 29, 1937, does not mean the same thing that it meant on Monday, June 1, 1936." The head of one of the railway brotherhoods carried that thought a step further in noting, "On Easter Sunday, state minimum wage laws were unconstitutional, but about noon on Easter Monday, these laws were constitutional." That development perturbed some longtime critics of the Court ("What kind of respect do you think one can instill in law students for the process of the Court when things like this can happen?" Felix Frankfurter asked) but gave others no little satisfaction. A former United States senator from West Virginia wrote: "Suppose you have noticed that the untouchables, the infallible, sacrosanct Supreme Court judges have been forced to put upon the record that they are just a bundle of flesh and blood, and must walk upon the ground like the rest of human beings. I got quite a 'kick' out of reading that the Supreme Court said, right out loud in meeting, that it had been wrong. Like most of the wrongs done in life, there is no compensation for the great wrongs which that old court has been doing the country; but like all democrats, I am forgiving."

The performance of the Court proved especially embarrassing for the Chief Justice. Commentators, observing that Hughes had once said of a nineteenth-century decision that the "over-ruling in such a short time by one vote, of the previous decision, shook popular respect for the Court," pointed out that "now, within a period of only ten months, the Supreme Court had reversed itself on minimum wages, again by one vote." To be sure, Hughes did not admit that the Court had shifted, and years later Roberts claimed that he had voted with the Four Horsemen in *Tipaldo* only because New York had not presented the issue in the right manner. Furthermore, we now know that in *Parrish* Roberts had not been responding to the Court-packing threat since he had cast his vote before the plan was announced. However, scholars, who have the advantage of information not generally known in 1937, find Roberts's contention that he did not switch unpersuasive.

At the time, no one doubted that the Court, and more particularly Mr. Justice Roberts, had crossed over. "Isn't everything today exciting?" wrote one of the women who led the National Consumers' League. "Just to think that silly Roberts should have the power to play politics and decide the fate of Minimum Wage legislation. But, thank God he thought it was politically expedient to be with us." In a more whimsical vein, *The New Yorker* remarked: "We are told that the Supreme Court's about-face was not due to outside clamor. It seems that the new building has a soundproof room, to which justices may retire to change their minds."

Yet despite all the ridicule directed at the Court, Hughes read the opinion in Elsie Parrish's case with an unmistakable note of exultation in his voice. For by being able to show that he had won Roberts to his side in *Parrish*, he had gone a long way toward defeating the Court-packing scheme. Once Roosevelt had a 5-4 majority for social legislation, there no longer appeared to be an urgent need for a drastic remedy. "Why," it was asked, "shoot the bridegroom after a shotgun wedding?" Not for nearly four months would FDR's proposal be finally rejected, and it would retain substantial backing almost to the very end, but never was it as formidable a proposition as it had been on the eve of Elsie Parrish's case. Within days after the decision was handed down, Washington insiders were regaling one another with a saucy sentence that encapsulated the new legislative situation: "A switch in time saved nine."

## The Constitutional Revolution of 1937

The Court's shift in *Parrish* proved to be the first of many. On the very day that *Parrish* was decided, "White Monday," the Court also upheld a revised farm mortgage law (the original one had been struck down on "Black Monday," in 1935) as well as other reform statutes. Two weeks later, once more by 5-4 with Roberts in the majority, it validated the Wagner Act (the National Labor Relations Act) and in the following month it turned aside challenges to the Social Security Act. Indeed, never again did the Supreme Court strike down a New Deal law, and from 1937 to the present it has not overturned a single piece of significant national or state legislation establishing minimal labor standards. Many commentators even believe that the Court has forever abandoned its power of judicial review in this field. Little wonder then that analysts speak of the "Constitutional Revolution of 1937."

Battle-scarred veterans of the minimum wage movement found themselves in a universe remade. The seventeen states with minimum wage statutes on their books now took steps to enforce them, and New York made plans to enact new legislation to replace the law struck down in *Tipaldo*. Even more consequential were the implications of *Parrish* for the national government. Late in 1936 President Roosevelt had told newspapermen of an experience on the streets of New Bedford when his campaign car was mobbed by enthusiastic well-wishers, twenty thousand of them crowded into a space intended to hold a thousand:

> "There was a girl six or seven feet away who was trying to pass an envelope to me and she was just too far away to reach. One of the policemen threw her back into the crowd and I said to my driver 'Get the note from that girl.' He got

it and handed it to me and the note said this ... 'Dear Mr. President: I wish you could do something to help us girls. You are the only recourse we have got left. We have been working in a sewing factory ... and up to a few months ago we were getting our minimum pay of $11 a week. ... Today the 200 of us girls have been cut down to $4 and $5 and $6 a week. You are the only man that can do anything about it. Please send somebody from Washington up here to restore our minimum wages because we cannot live on $4 or $5 or $6 a week.'

"That is something that so many of us found in the Campaign, that these people think that I have the power to restore things like minimum wages and maximum hours and the elimination of child labor. ... And, of course, I haven't any power to do it."

Now, thanks to the constitutional revolution that the Wenatchee chambermaid had detonated, Congress was able to give him that power, and when the Fair Labor Standards Act of 1938 that set minimum wages and maximum hours for both men and women was challenged in the courts, a reconstituted Supreme Court found no difficulty in validating it.

Long before then Elsie Parrish had faded into the anonymity from which she had risen, and when more than thirty-five years later Adela Rogers St. Johns, a reporter who had won renown as the "sob sister" of the Hearst press, tracked her down in Anaheim, California, Mrs. Parrish expressed surprise that anyone would pay attention to her. Surrounded by grandchildren, looking much younger than her years, "dressed in something pink and fresh-washed and ironed," she said that she had gotten little notice at the time and "none of the women running around yelling about Lib and such have paid any since." But she was quietly confident that she had accomplished something of historic significance—less for herself than for all the thousands of women scrubbing floors in hotels, toiling at laundry vats, and tending machines in factories who needed to know that, however belatedly, they could summon the law to their side.

# CHAPTER 3

# Denying Fair Labor Standards and Upholding States' Rights

# Case Overview

## National League of Cities v. Usery (1976)

When the Fair Labor Standards Act (FLSA) was passed in 1938, it allowed Congress to impose minimum wage standards on private businesses engaged in interstate commerce. State and city workers were explicitly excluded. So, for example, while Congress could require a private school to pay its teachers a certain wage, it could not make such a demand on a public school. Over the years, the FLSA was amended many times, and each time Congress was given greater power to regulate states' economic affairs. The expansionist trend stopped in 1975, when the case of *National League of Cities v. Usery* first came before the Supreme Court.

A 1974 federal statue allowed Congress to regulate not only private labor arrangements but those of state and city employees as well. In response, the National League of Cities, together with the National Governors Conference and several state and city governments, brought a court action in the District of Columbia against the U.S. secretary of labor, W.J. Usery Jr. The appellants argued that the Constitution does not explicitly grant Congress the power to regulate state employees not engaged in interstate commerce. Furthermore, according to the Tenth Amendment, powers not expressly delegated to the federal government in the Constitution belong to the states. Thus, Congress has no authority to tell states how much to pay their workers.

The district court ruled in favor of the defendants but was concerned that the amended FLSA would have the effect of preventing states from carrying out their "essential" functions, such as providing police or fire services. Consequently, the court recommended that the Supreme Court hear the case to determine whether the commerce clause of the Constitution really gave this much power to Congress. The question presented to the Court was whether the Tenth Amendment prohibits Congress, acting under its commerce powers, from trying to regulate the labor market of state employees.

The Supreme Court did, indeed, change its mind. Whereas the Court had ruled that Congress had a constitutional right to set minimum wage levels for state employees, the Court now overturned its earlier ruling. Writing for the majority in 1976, Justice William Rehnquist argued that Congress may not use its commerce powers to tell states how to perform "essential" functions. What counts as an essential function? Rehnquist classed "traditional" state functions, like police and fire protection, as essential. He reasoned that federal wage and hour laws interfere so much with states' decisions about how they will provide these services that there is nothing left for states to do. If Congress revoked states' authority to make such "fundamental employment decisions," Rehnquist continued, states would barely continue to exist as independent political entities.

In his dissent, Justice John Paul Stevens suggested that Rehnquist's definition of "essential function" was arbitrary and misleading. Stevens described a variety of ways the federal government regulates state employees, even while they are performing essential state functions. Though Stevens himself doubted the wisdom of minimum wage legislation, he could find no principle that would bar Congress from passing wage laws for state employees.

*The National League of Cities v. Usery* was the first Supreme Court decision in forty years to restrict federal commerce powers, thereby increasing states' authority to set wage levels. Its test for defining the boundaries of state and federal wage-setting powers, however, was controversial, and in *Garcia v. San Antonio Metropolitan Transit Authority* (1985), the Court ruled that Congress did have the authority to set minimum wage levels for state employees.

> *"One undoubted attribute of state sovereignty is the States' power to determine the wages which shall be paid to those whom they employ in order to carry out their governmental functions."*

# Majority Opinion: Federal Minimum Wage Requirements Violate States' Sovereignty

*William Rehnquist*

*William Rehnquist was nominated by President Richard Nixon to the Supreme Court in 1971. After serving as an associate justice for fifteen years, he was nominated in 1986 by President Ronald Reagan to be chief justice of the United States. He wrote the majority opinion in the case of* National League of Cities v. Usery *(1976), wherein the Court struck down a 1974 federal statute that extended the maximum hours and minimum wage provisions of the Fair Labor Standards Act (FLSA) to most state and municipal employees. In the case, the National League of Cities contended that the 1974 amendments of the FLSA violated the Tenth Amendment to the Constitution. The Court agreed with the appellants, with Rehnquist arguing that the new FLSA amendments impinged upon state sovereignty.*

Nearly 40 year[s] ago, Congress enacted the Fair Labor Standards Act, and required employers covered by the Act to pay their employees a minimum hourly wage and to pay them at one and one-half time their regular rate of pay

William Rehnquist, majority opinion, *National League of Cities v. Usery*, U.S. Supreme Court, 1976.

for hours worked in excess of 40 during a workweek. By this Act, covered employers were required to keep certain records to aid in the enforcement of the Act, and to comply with specified child labor standards. This Court unanimously upheld the Act as a valid exercise of congressional authority under the commerce power in *United States v. Darby* (1941).

## Broadening of the FLSA

In a series of amendments beginning in 1961, Congress began to extend the provisions of the Fair Labor Standards Act to some types of public employees. The 1961 amendments to the Act extended its coverage to persons who were employed in "enterprises" engaged in commerce or in the production of goods for commerce. And in 1966, with the amendment of the definition of employers under the Act, the exemption heretofore extended to the States and their political subdivisions was removed with respect to employees of state hospitals, institutions, and schools. We nevertheless sustained the validity of the combined effect of these two amendments in *Maryland v. Wirtz* (1968).

In 1974, Congress again broadened the coverage of the Act. The definition of "employer" in the Act now specifically "includes a public agency." In addition, the critical definition of "[e]nterprise[s] engaged in commerce or in the production of goods for commerce" was expanded to encompass "an activity of a public agency." . . .

By its 1974 amendments, then, Congress has now entirely removed the exemption previously afforded States and their political subdivisions, substituting only the Act's general exemption for executive, administrative, or professional personnel, which is supplemented by provisions excluding from the Act's coverage those individuals holding public elective office or serving such an officeholder in one of several specific capacities. The Act thus imposes upon almost all public employment the minimum wage and maximum hour requirements previously restricted to employees engaged in interstate commerce. These requirements are essentially identical to those imposed upon private employers, although the Act does attempt to make some provision for public employment relationships which are without counterpart in the private sector, such as those presented by fire protection and law enforcement personnel. . . .

## Congressional Authority and State Sovereignty

It is established beyond peradventure that the Commerce Clause of Art. I of the Constitution is a grant of plenary authority to Congress. That authority is, in the words of Mr. Chief Justice [John] Marshall in *Gibbons v. Ogden* (1824), "the power to regulate; that is, to prescribe the rule by which commerce is to be governed." . . .

This Court has never doubted that there are limits upon the power of Congress to override state sovereignty, even when exercising its otherwise plenary powers to tax or to regulate commerce which are conferred by Art. I of the Constitution. In *Wirtz*, for example, the Court took care to assure the appellants that it had "ample power to prevent . . . 'the utter destruction of the State as a sovereign political entity,'" which they feared. Appellee Secretary in this case, both in his brief and upon oral argument, has agreed that our federal system of government imposes definite limits upon the authority of Congress to regulate the activities of the States as States by means of the commerce power. . . .

Appellee Secretary argues that the cases in which this Court has upheld sweeping exercises of authority by Congress, even though those exercises preempted state regulation of the private sector, have already curtailed the sovereignty of the States quite as much as the 1974 amendments to the Fair Labor Standards Act. We do not agree. It is one thing to recognize the authority of Congress to enact laws regulating individual businesses necessarily subject to the dual sovereignty of the government of the Nation and of the State in which they reside. It is quite another to uphold a similar exercise of congressional authority directed not to private citizens, but to the States as States. We have repeatedly recognized that there are attributes of sovereignty attaching to every state government which may not be impaired by Congress, not because Congress may lack an affirmative grant of legislative authority to reach the matter, but because the Constitution prohibits it from exercising the authority in that manner.

One undoubted attribute of state sovereignty is the States' power to determine the wages which shall be paid to those whom they employ in order to carry out their governmental functions, what hours those persons will work, and what compensation will be provided where these employees may be called upon to work overtime. The question we must resolve here, then, is whether these determinations are "'functions essential to separate and independent existence,'" so that Congress may not abrogate the States' otherwise plenary authority to make them.

## Costs Impact Government Function

In their complaint, appellants advanced estimates of substantial costs which will be imposed upon them by the 1974 amendments. Since the District Court dismissed their complaint, we take its well pleaded allegations as true, although it appears from appellee's submissions in the District Court and in this Court that resolution of the factual disputes as to the effect of the amendments is not critical to our disposition of the case.

Judged solely in terms of increased costs in dollars, these allegation[s] show a significant impact on the functioning of the governmental bodies involved. The Metropolitan Government of Nashville and Davidson County, Tenn., for example, asserted that the Act will increase its costs of providing essential police and fire protection, without any increase in service or in current salary levels, by $938,000 per year. Cape Girardeau, Mo., estimated that its annual budget for fire protection may have to be increased by anywhere from $250,000 to $400,000 over the current figure of $350,000. The State of Arizona alleged that the annual additional expenditures which will be required if it is to continue to provide essential state services may total $2.5 million. The State of California, which must devote significant portions of its budget to fire suppression endeavors, estimated that application of the Act to its employment practices will necessitate an increase in its budget of between $8 million and $16 million.

Increased costs are not, of course, the only adverse effects which compliance with the Act will visit upon state and local governments, and, in turn, upon the citizens who depend upon those governments. In its complaint in intervention, for example, California asserted that it could not comply with the overtime costs (approximately $750,000 per year) which the Act required to be paid to California Highway Patrol cadets during their academy training program. California reported that it had thus been forced to reduce its academy training program from 2,080 hours to only 960 hours, a compromise undoubtedly of substantial importance to those whose safety and welfare may depend upon the preparedness of the California Highway Patrol.

This type of forced relinquishment of important governmental activities is further reflected in the complaint's allegation that the city of Inglewood, Cal., has been forced to curtail its affirmative action program for providing employment opportunities for men and women interested in a career in law enforcement. The Inglewood police department has abolished a program for police trainees who split their week between on-the-job training and the classroom. The city could not abrogate its contractual obligations to these trainees, and it concluded that compliance with the Act in these circumstances was too financially burdensome to permit continuance of the classroom program. The city of Clovis, Cal., has been put to a similar choice regarding an internship program it was running in cooperation with a California State university. According to the complaint, because the interns' compensation brings them within the purview of the Act, the city must decide whether to eliminate the program entirely or to substantially reduce its beneficial aspects by doing away with any pay for the interns.

## Impact on State Policies

Quite apart from the substantial costs imposed upon the States and their political subdivisions, the Act displaces state policies regarding the manner in which they will structure delivery of those governmental services which their citizens require. The Act, speaking directly to the States *qua*[as] States, requires that they shall pay all but an extremely limited minority of their employees the minimum wage rate currently chosen by Congress. It may well be that, as a matter of economic policy, it would be desirable that States, just as private employers, comply with these minimum wage requirement. But it cannot be gainsaid that the federal requirement directly supplant the considered policy choice of the States' elected officials and administrators as to how they wish to structure pay scale in state employment. The State might wish to employ persons with little or no training, or those who wish to work on a casual basis, or those who, for some other reason, do not possess minimum employment requirements, and pay them less than the federally prescribed minimum wage. It may wish to offer part-time or summer employment to teenagers at a figure less than the minimum wage, and, if unable to do so, may decline to offer such employment at all. But the Act would forbid such choice by the States. The only "discretion" left to them under the Act is either to attempt to increase their revenue to meet the additional financial burden imposed upon them by paying Congressionally prescribed wages to their existing complement of employees or to reduce that complement to a number which can be paid the federal minimum wage without increasing revenue.

This dilemma presented by the minimum wage restriction may seem not immediately different from that faced by private employers, who have long been covered by the Act and who must find ways to increase their gross income if they are to pay higher wages while maintaining current earnings. The difference, however, is that a State is not merely a factor in the "shifting economic arrangements" of the private sector of the economy, *Kovacs v. Cooper* (1949), but is itself a coordinate element in the system established by the Framers for governing our Federal Union.

## Separate and Independent Existence

The degree to which the FLSA amendments would interfere with traditional aspects of state sovereignty can be seen even more clearly upon examining the overtime requirements of the Act. The general effect of these provisions is to require the States to pay their employees at premium rates whenever their work exceeds a specified number of hours in a given period. The asserted reason for these provisions is to provide a financial disincentive upon using employees beyond the work period deemed appropriate by Congress. . . .

But, like the minimum wage provisions, the vice of the Act as sought to be applied here is that it directly penalizes the States for choosing to hire governmental employees on terms different from those which Congress has sought to impose. . . .

Our examination of the effect of the 1974 amendments, as sought to be extended to the States and their political subdivisions, satisfies us that both the minimum wage and the maximum hour provisions will impermissibly interfere with the integral governmental functions of these bodies. We earlier noted some disagreement between the parties regarding the precise effect the amendments will have in application. We do not believe particularized assessments of actual impact are crucial to resolution of the issue presented, however. For even if we accept appellee's assessments concerning the impact of the amendments, their application will nonetheless significantly alter or displace the States' abilities to structure employer/ employee relationships in such areas as fire prevention, police protection, sanitation, public health, and parks and recreation. These activities are typical of those performed by state and local governments in discharging their dual functions of administering the public law and furnishing public services. Indeed, it is functions such as these which governments are created to provide, services such as these which the States have traditionally afforded their citizens. If Congress may withdraw from the States the authority to make those fundamental employment decisions upon which their systems for performance of these functions must rest, we think there would be little left of the States' "'separate and independent existence.'" Thus, even if appellants may have overestimated the effect which the Act will have upon their current levels and patterns of governmental activity, the dispositive factor is that Congress has attempted to exercise its Commerce Clause authority to prescribe minimum wages and maximum hours to be paid by the States in their capacities as sovereign governments. In so doing, Congress has sought to wield its power in a fashion that would impair the States' "ability to function effectively in a federal system." This exercise of congressional authority does not comport with the federal system of government embodied in the Constitution. We hold that, insofar as the challenged amendments operate to directly displace the States' freedom to structure integral operations in areas of traditional governmental functions, they are not within the authority granted Congress.

## *Fry* and *Wirtz* as Precedents

One final matter requires our attention. Appellee has vigorously urged that we cannot, consistently with the Court's decisions in *Maryland v. Wirtz*, and *Fry* [ *v. United States*], rule against him here. It is important to examine this contention so that it will be clear what we hold today, and what we do not. With regard to *Fry*, we disagree with appellee. There, the Court held that the Economic Stabilization Act of 1970 was constitutional as applied to temporarily freeze the wages of state and local government employees. The Court expressly noted that the degree of intrusion upon the protected area of state sovereignty was in that case even less than that worked by the amendments to the FLSA which were before the Court in *Wirtz*. The Court recognized that the Economic Stabilization Act was "an emergency measure to counter severe inflation that threatened the national economy."

We think our holding today quite consistent with *Fry*. The enactment at issue there was occasioned by an extremely serious problem which endangered the well-being of all the component parts of our federal system and which only collective action by the National Government might forestall. The means selected were carefully drafted so as not to interfere with the States' freedom beyond a very limited, specific period of time. The effect of the across-the-board freeze authorized by that Act, moreover, displaced no state choices as to how governmental operations should be structured, nor did it force the States to remake such choices themselves. Instead, it merely required that the wage scales and employment relationships which the States themselves had chosen be maintained during the period of the emergency. Finally, the Economic Stabilization Act operated to reduce the pressures upon state budgets, rather than increase them. These factors distinguish the statute in *Fry* from the provisions at issue here. The limits imposed upon the commerce power when Congress seeks to apply it to the States are not so inflexible as to preclude temporary enactments tailored to combat a national emergency. . . .

With respect to the Court's decision in *Wirtz*, we reach a different conclusion. Both appellee and the District Court thought that decision required rejection of appellants' claims. Appellants, in turn, advance several arguments by which they seek to distinguish the facts before the Court in *Wirtz* from those presented by the 1974 amendments to the Act. There are undoubtedly factual distinctions between the two situations, but, in view of the conclusions expressed earlier in this opinion, we do not believe the reasoning in *Wirtz* may any longer be regarded as authoritative.

## Congress Cannot Dictate State Decisions

But we have reaffirmed today that the States, as States, stand on a quite different footing from an individual or a corporation when challenging the exercise of Congress' power to regulate commerce. We think the dicta [judges' expressed opinions that are not applicable to the case being tried.] from *United States v. California* simply wrong. Congress may not exercise that power so as to force directly upon the States its choices as to how essential decisions regarding the conduct of integral governmental functions are to be made. We agree that such assertions of power, if unchecked, would indeed, as Mr. Justice [William] Douglas cautioned in his dissent in *Wirtz*, allow "the National Government [to] devour the essentials of state sovereignty" and would therefore transgress the bounds of the authority granted Congress under the Commerce Clause. While there are obvious differences between the schools and hospitals involved in *Wirtz*, and the fire and police departments affected here, each provides an integral portion of those governmental services which the States and their political subdivisions have traditionally afforded their citizens. We are therefore persuaded that *Wirtz* must be overruled.

The judgment of the District Court is accordingly reversed, and the cases are remanded for further proceedings consistent with this opinion.

*"We are left [by the Court's decision] with a catastrophic judicial body blow at Congress' power."*

# Dissenting Opinion: The Court's Decision Is a Blow to Congressional Power

*William J. Brennan Jr.*

*William J. Brennan Jr. was appointed to the Supreme Court in 1956 by President Dwight D. Eisenhower and served until 1990. In his dissenting opinion in* National League of Cities v. Usery *he offers a harsh criticism of the majority decision, contending that the Court, in striking down a statute requiring states to be subject to minimum wage and maximum hours provisions, "manufactured an abstraction" with no basis in the Constitution. The Court decided that Congress, even acting under the commerce clause of the Constitution, may not regulate the labor market of state employees, because the Tenth Amendment reserves such regulation to the states. Brennan describes previous cases in which the Court deferred to congressional regulation in the commerce area, citing earlier decisions in which state sovereignty is limited by federal power. He charges that the majority seeks to invalidate particular congressional judgment based on ideological differences and thus are guilty of violating the principles of judicial restraint. He laments the decision as a catastrophic blow to Congress's power.*

William J. Brennan Jr., dissenting opinion, *National League of Cities v. Usery*, U.S. Supreme Court, 1976.

My Brethren do not successfully obscure today's patent usurpation of the role reserved for the political process by their purported discovery in the Constitution of a restraint derived from sovereignty of the States on Congress' exercise of the commerce power. Mr. Chief Justice [John] Marshall recognized that limitations "prescribed in the constitution" restrain Congress' exercise of the power. Thus, laws within the commerce power may not infringe individual liberties protected by the First Amendment; the Fifth Amendment; or the Sixth Amendment. But there is no restraint based on state sovereignty requiring or permitting judicial enforcement anywhere expressed in the Constitution; our decisions over the last century and a half have explicitly rejected the existence of any such restraint on the commerce power. . . .

My Brethren thus have today manufactured an abstraction without substance, founded neither in the words of the Constitution nor on precedent. An abstraction having such profoundly pernicious consequences is not made less so by characterizing the 1974 amendments as legislation directed against the "States *qua*[as] States." Of course, regulations that this Court can say are not regulations of "commerce" cannot stand, and, in this sense, "[t]he Court has ample power to prevent . . . 'the utter destruction of the State as a sovereign political entity.'" But my Brethren make no claim that the 1974 amendments are not regulations of "commerce"; rather, they overrule *Wirtz* in disagreement with historic principles that *United States v. California* reaffirmed. . . .

## No Restraint of Commerce Power

The reliance of my Brethren upon the Tenth Amendment as "an express declaration of limitation [of a state's sovereignty]" not only suggests that they overrule governing decisions of this Court that address this question but must astound scholars of the Constitution. . . .

My Brethren purport to find support for their novel state sovereignty doctrine in the concurring opinion of Mr. Chief Justice [Harlan] Stone in *New York v. United States* (1946). That reliance is plainly misplaced. That case presented the question whether the Constitution either required immunity of New York State's mineral water business from federal taxation or denied to the Federal Government power to lay the tax. The Court sustained the federal tax. . . .

In contrast, the apposite decision . . . to the question whether the Constitution implies a state sovereignty restraint upon congressional exercise of the commerce power is *Case v. Bowles* (1946). The question there was whether the Emergency Price Control Act could apply to the sale by the State of Washington of timber growing on lands granted by Congress to the State for the support of common schools. The State contended that

> there is a doctrine implied in the Federal Constitution that "the two governments, national and state, are each to exercise its powers so as not to interfere with the free and full exercise of the powers of the other" . . . , [and] that the Act cannot be applied to this sale because it was "for the purpose of gaining revenue to carry out an essential governmental function—the education of its citizens."

The Court emphatically rejected that argument. . . .

Even more significant for our purposes is the Court's citation of *United States v. California*, a case concerned with Congress' power to regulate commerce, as supporting the rejection of the State's contention that state sovereignty is a limitation on Congress' war power. California directly presented the question whether any state sovereignty restraint precluded application of the Federal Safety Appliance Act to a state owned and operated railroad. . . .

Mr. Justice Stone rejected the contention in an opinion for a unanimous Court. . . .

## Unjustified Rejection of Precedent

Today's repudiation of this unbroken line of precedent that firmly reject my Brethren's ill-conceived abstraction can only be regarded as a transparent cover or invalidating a congressional judgment with which they disagree. The only analysis even remotely resembling that adopted today is found in a line of opinions dealing with the Commerce Clause and the Tenth Amendment that ultimately provoked a constitutional crisis for the Court in the 1930's. *E.g., Carter v. Carter Coal Co.* (1936); *United States v. Butler* (1936); *Hammer v. Dagenhart* (1918). We tend to forget that the Court invalidated legislation during the Great Depression not solely under the Due Process Clause, but also and primarily under the Commerce Clause and the Tenth Amendment. It may have been the eventual abandonment of that overly restrictive construction of the commerce power that spelled defeat for the Court packing plan [of President F.D. Roosevelt], and preserved the integrity of this institution, but my Brethren today are transparently trying to cut back on that recognition of the scope of the commerce power. My Brethren's approach to this case is not far different from the dissenting opinions in the cases that averted the crisis.

That no precedent justifies today's result is particularly clear from the awkward extension of the doctrine of state immunity from federal taxation—an immunity conclusively distinguished by Mr. Justice Stone in California, and an immunity that is "narrowly limited" because "the people of all the states have created the national government and are represented in Congress," to fashion a judicially enforceable restraint on Congress' exercise of the commerce power that the Court has time and again rejected as having no place in our constitutional jurisprudence. . . .

My Brethren's treatment of *Fry v. United States* (1975), further illustrates the paucity of legal reasoning or principle justifying today's result. Although the Economic Stabilization Act "displace[d] the States' freedom,"—the reason given for invalidating the 1974 amendments—the result in *Fry* is not disturbed, since the interference was temporary, and only a national program enforced by the Federal Government could have alleviated the country's economic crisis. Thus, although my Brethren, by fiat, strike down the 1974 amendments without analysis of countervailing national considerations, *Fry*, by contrary logic, remains undisturbed, because, on balance, countervailing national considerations override the interference with the State's freedom. Moreover, it is sophistry to say the Economic Stabilization Act "displaced no state choices," but that the 1974 amendments do. Obviously the Stabilization Act—no less than every exercise of a national power delegated to Congress by the Constitution—displaced the State's freedom. It is absurd to suggest that there is a constitutionally significant distinction between curbs against increasing wages and curbs against paying wages lower than the federal minimum.

## State Sovereignty vs. Federal Regulatory Powers

Today's holding patently is in derogation of the sovereign power of the Nation to regulate interstate commerce. Can the States engage in businesses competing with the private sector and then come to the courts arguing that withdrawing the employees of those businesses from the private sector evades the power of the Federal Government to regulate commerce? No principle given meaningful content by my Brethren today precludes the States from doing just that. Our historic decisions rejecting all suggestions that the States stand in a different position from affected private parties when challenging congressional exercise of the commerce power reflect that very concern. . . .

Also devoid of meaningful content is my Brethren's argument that the 1974 amendments "displac[e] State policies." The amendments neither impose policy objectives on the States nor deny the States complete freedom to fix their own objectives. My Brethren boldly assert that the decision as to wages and hours is an "undoubted attribute of state sovereignty," and then never say why. Indeed, they disclaim any reliance on the costs of compliance with the amendments in reaching today's result. This would enable my Brethren to conclude that, however insignificant that cost, any federal regulation under the commerce power "will nonetheless significantly alter or displace the States' abilities to structure employer/employee relationships." This then would mean that, whether or not state wages are paid for the performance of an "essential" state function (whatever that may mean), the newly discovered state sovereignty constraint could operate as a flat and absolute prohibition against congressional regulation of the wages and hours of state employees under the Commerce Clause. The portent of such a sweeping holding is so ominous for our constitutional jurisprudence as to leave one incredulous.

Certainly the paradigm of sovereign action—action *qua* State—is in the enactment and enforcement of state laws. Is it possible that my Brethren are signaling abandonment of the heretofore unchallenged principle that Congress "can, if it chooses, entirely displace the States to the full extent of the far-reaching Commerce Clause"? Indeed, that principle sometimes invalidates state laws regulating subject matter of national importance even when Congress has been silent. In either case, the ouster of state laws obviously curtails or prohibits the States' prerogatives to make policy choices respecting subjects clearly of greater significance to the "State *qua* State" than the minimum wage paid to state employees. The Supremacy Clause dictates this result under "the federal system of government embodied in the Constitution."

## The Restructuring of Government

My Brethren do more than turn aside longstanding constitutional jurisprudence that emphatically rejects today's conclusion. More alarming is the startling restructuring of our federal system, and the role they create therein for the federal judiciary. This Court is simply not at liberty to erect a mirror of its own conception of a desirable governmental structure. If the 1974 amendments have any "vice," my Brother [John Paul] Stevens is surely right that it represents "merely . . . a policy issue which has been firmly resolved by the branches of government having power to decide such questions." It bears repeating "that effective restraints on . . . exercise [of the commerce power] must proceed from political, rather than from judicial, processes."

It is unacceptable that the judicial process should be thought superior to the political process in this area. Under the Constitution, the Judiciary has no role to play beyond finding that Congress has not made an unreasonable legislative judgment respecting what is "commerce." My Brother [Harry] Blackmun suggests that controlling judicial supervision of the relationship between the States and our National Government by use of a balancing approach diminishes the ominous implications of today's decision. Such an approach, however, is a thinly veiled rationalization for judicial supervision of a policy judgment that our system of government reserves to Congress.

Judicial restraint in this area merely recognizes that the political branches of our Government are structured to protect the interests of the States, as well as the Nation as a whole, and that the States are fully able to protect their own interests in the premises. Congress is constituted of representatives in both the Senate and House elected from the States. . . . There is no reason whatever to suppose that, in enacting the 1974 amendments, Congress, even if it might extensively obliterate state sovereignty by fully exercising its plenary power respecting commerce, had any purpose to do so. Surely the presumption must be to the contrary. Any realistic assessment of our federal political system, dominated as it is by representatives of the people elected from the States, yields the conclusion that it is highly unlikely that those representatives will ever be motivated to disregard totally the concerns of these States. . . .

A sense of the enormous impact of States' political power is gained by brief reference to the federal budget. The largest estimate by any of the appellants of the cost impact of the 1974 amendments—$1 billion—pales in comparison with the financial assistance the States receive from the Federal Government. In fiscal 1977, the President's proposed budget recommends $60.5 billion in federal assistance to the States, exclusive of loans. . . . Appellants complain of the impact of the amended FLSA [Fair Labor Standards Act] on police and fire departments, but the 1977 budget contemplates outlays for law enforcement assistance of $716 million. Concern is also expressed about the diminished ability to hire students in the summer if States must pay them a minimum wage, but the Federal Government's "summer youth program" provides $400 million for 670,000 jobs. Given this demonstrated ability to obtain funds from the Federal Government for needed state services, there is little doubt that the States' influence in the political process is adequate to safeguard their sovereignty.

My Brethren's disregard for precedents recognizing these long-settled constitutional principles is painfully obvious in their cavalier treatment of *Maryland v. Wirtz*. . . .

No effort is made to distinguish the FLSA amendments sustained in *Wirtz* from the 1974 amendments. We are told at the outset that "the 'far-reaching implications' of *Wirtz* should be overruled;" later it is said that the "reasoning in *Wirtz*" is no longer "authoritative". My Brethren then merely restate their essential function test, and say that *Wirtz* must "therefore" be overruled. There is no analysis [of] whether *Wirtz* reached the correct result, apart from any flaws in reasoning, even though we are told that "there are obvious differences" between this case and *Wirtz*. Are state and federal interests being silently balanced, as in the discussion of *Fry*? The best I can make of it is that the 1966 FLSA amendments are struck down and *Wirtz* is overruled on the basis of the conceptually unworkable essential function test, and that the test is unworkable is demonstrated by my Brethren's inability to articulate any meaningful distinctions among state-operated railroads, state-operated schools and hospitals, and state-operated police and fire departments.

We are left then with a catastrophic judicial body blow at Congress' power under the Commerce Clause. Even if Congress may nevertheless accomplish its objectives—for example, by conditioning grants of federal funds upon compliance with federal minimum wage and overtime standards—there is an ominous portent of disruption of our constitutional structure implicit in today's mischievous decision.

"The [Court's] decision . . . offers surprising support for a claim on behalf of
[personal] rights."

# National League of Cities Does Not Restrict Personal Rights

*Laurence H. Tribe*

*Laurence H. Tribe, a professor at Harvard Law School, is re-
garded as one of the foremost constitutional law experts in the
United States. In his analysis of* National League of Cities v.
Usery, *he argues that while the case has come to symbolize the
federalism of the Warren Burger Supreme Court, it is more properly seen as a decision that sought to provide states with the
means to provide the basic services guaranteed by the Constitution. The National League of Cities claimed that the 1974 statute requiring them to conform to minimum wage and maximum hours standards outlined in the Fair Labor Standards Act
(FLSA) violated their Tenth Amendment rights. The Court found
for the plaintiff, agreeing that Congress overstepped its authority
by dictating states' labor practices. Tribe says that many commentators have seen the decision as one that restricts personal
rights, but in truth it supports such rights. From a logical point
of view, he argues, not restricting states' labor practices would
have the effect of allowing them to provide their citizens with the
affirmative rights—to basic services that are essential to their existence—that are necessary in a just constitutional order.*

Laurence H. Tribe, "Unraveling 'National League of Cities': The New Federalism and Affirmative Rights to Essential Government Services," *Harvard Law Review*, vol. 90, April
1977, pp. 1065–70, 1078–79, 1086–87, 1102–04. Copyright © 1977 by Harvard Law Review Association. Republished with permission of Harvard Law Review, conveyed
through Copyright Clearance Center, Inc.

No great acumen is required to detect in recent decisions of the United States Supreme Court a retreat from the vigorous defense of liberty and equality. The primary victims of this shift in judicial attitude have been our society's oppressed; its clearest beneficiaries have not been among those in special need of judicial assistance. I believe that eventually the period through which we are passing will be marked not as the end of an era of misguided activism but as an unhappy pause in our progress toward a just society. In particular, I am convinced that, despite its difficulties, a doctrine will ultimately emerge that recognizes under the fifth and fourteenth amendments constitutional rights to decent levels of affirmative governmental protection in meeting the basic human needs of physical survival and security, health and housing, employment and education. The time will come when constitutional law will answer the scholar's question, "Why education and not golf?" with the only reply that makes human sense—"Because education is more important"—and when this answer, however odd it will seem to some lawyers, will seem convincing to those who take their lessons from life itself.

I say all of this at the outset in order to put this [viewpoint] in context. For I will be discussing here one of the Supreme Court decisions, *National League of Cities v. Usery*, that could most easily be identified with the general move to restrict personal rights. But I will be arguing that the decision instead offers surprising support for a claim on behalf of such rights. Let me therefore be clear from the beginning about the character of my thesis. I make no claims about what the Justices intended or "really had in mind." I haven't a clue what that might have been, but I doubt that the conclusion of this [viewpoint] was it. I will be arguing about the logic, not the motives, of the Court's action. And I will be arguing about that logic with a purpose of my own: to enlist that logic—

while remaining faithful to its premises—in the search, perhaps delayed but not defeated, for a just constitutional order.

## The Court's Federalism

[In 1976] for the first time in four decades, the Supreme Court held a congressional regulation of commerce to be an unconstitutional intrusion upon the sovereignty of state and local governments. In *National League of Cities v. Usery*, the Court invalidated the 1974 amendments to the Fair Labor Standards Act (FLSA) which had extended federal minimum wage and maximum hour provisions to almost all state and municipal employees. In reaching its conclusion, the Court sharply distinguished federal regulation of private persons and businesses "necessarily subject to the dual sovereignty of the government of the Nation and of the State in which they reside" from similar regulation "directed not to private citizens, but to the States as States." Although the Court conceded that the regulations at issue were "undoubtedly within the scope of the Commerce Clause," it found that wage and hour determinations with respect to "functions ... which [state and local] governments are created to provide, [involving] services ... which the States have traditionally afforded their citizens," were matters "essential to separate and independent existence" of the states and hence beyond the reach of congressional power under the commerce clause.

Although the decision in *National League of Cities* startled some, its rhetoric of state sovereignty and local autonomy will doubtless seem to many others a natural extension of the concern for the rights of states in the federal system that the Court has recently emphasized. The Court's opinions have sounded such a note for several years, and the signals have recently become both louder and more frequent. The national mood, moreover, has increasingly been one of disenchantment with centralized power and a desire for local autonomy.

But to say that *National League of Cities* struck responsive chords in history and doctrine is not to say that the reasoning underlying the decision is easily understood or the result readily accepted. The very familiarity of the Court's federalism theme, coupled with the opinion's broad rhetoric, poses the danger that the decision will be read uncritically as a general vindication of the autonomy of states and municipalities, to the possible detriment of the rights of individuals. Understandable as such a response might be, it would be unwarranted. For despite the Court's tendency to invoke "federalism" as a restraint with little or no elucidation of its content, there is no reason this concept should resist clarification and no reason its invocation by the Court should be treated as an unanalyzable, albeit controversial, step in an inexorable march toward the restriction of federal power and the expansion of state authority. . . .

## Individual Rights

To view *National League of Cities* as a decision about individual rights might at first seem farfetched. While language may be quoted from the opinion—and arguments shaped from its reasoning—to support such a view, it remains true that the tenor of the opinion is one which is decidedly state-oriented. . . . It is worth noting that a focus on individual rights is hardly inconsistent with a concern for federalism. Since "[t]he federal and State governments are in fact but different agents and trustees of the people, constituted with different powers, and designed for different purposes," most of a state's "rights" must ultimately be derived from the rights of its citizens. And that the language of "states' rights" should be used to protect such individual rights against federal encroachment is certainly understandable when the federal government, in accord with national tradition, has left to the states the responsibility of vindicating the rights in question.

To be sure, neither *National League of Cities* nor any other recent decision provides a clear indication that the Supreme Court regards basic governmental services as constitutional rights of individuals. Yet the cases do not foreclose such an approach. On the contrary, the Court's reluctance to embrace arguments or express conclusions unambiguously eliminating any government obligation to provide basic services leads to a tension among rhetoric, reasoning, and results. That tension may well reflect an unarticulated perception that there exist constitutional norms establishing minimal entitlements to certain services—an intuitive sense that some expectations are protected. . . .

## Substantive Justice

Although the Supreme Court's decision in 1937 to overturn the *Lochner* line of cases and uphold maximum hour and minimum wage laws is typically perceived as a determination to defer to the political branches in socioeconomic matters, the seminal opinion in which the Court changed course, *West Coast Hotel Co. v. Parrish*, in fact spoke more of the substantive justice of minimum wage legislation than of the need to show institutional deference. Indeed, if one accepts fully one of the central notions contributing to *Lochner*'s demise—that even judicial enforcement of common law rules represents a governmental choice with concrete impacts on real persons—it becomes hard to avoid the realization that a judicial choice between sustaining and invalidating legislation altering the ground rules of contract and property is itself a positive, political choice—one guided by constitutional language and history, but almost never wholly determined by it. Having come to that realization, one must then recognize that a decision striking down a minimum wage law and a decision sustaining it both involve substantive choices; if the latter is right and the former wrong, the reason can only be that, in twentieth-century America, minimum wage laws are *not* intrusions upon human freedom in any meaningful sense but are instead entirely just ways of attempting to combat economic subjugation and human domination. Thus when the Court said in *West Coast Hotel Co. v. Parrish* that minimum wage laws, in light of "recent economic experience," prevented the "exploitation of ... workers," it was in effect concluding not simply that the "legislature was *entitled* to adopt measures to [raise] ... wages [too] low ... to meet the bare cost of living," but that the legislature was *right* to adopt such measures, although other ways of filling the gaps left by the state's fabric of private and public law were of course conceivable and have been pursued as entirely constitutional alternatives. . . .

The premises which led the Supreme Court to uphold as constitutional those limitations on contractual freedom thought necessary to provide decent living conditions for the underprivileged need not have been seen as premises of judicial passivity at all; understood with greater sensitivity to the human situation the Court was affecting, the same premises that toppled *Lochner* could propel courts to intervene actively in order to prevent governments from tolerating the extreme suffering and deprivation that was once "thought to be part of the natural hazards of life" but has since been perceived as "in fact attributable to the machinations of men." . . .

## The Court's Concern for Federalism

In order to make sense of *National League of Cities* and the distinctions the Court insisted on drawing in the course of that decision, we must recognize in the Court's concern for federalism a fear that, if state decisionmaking and the demands on state budgets are not sufficiently respected, certain individual rights to decent levels of basic government services, in such areas as public health, sanitation, and fire and police protection, might not be met. There has been ample irony in that conclusion, but it would be far more than ironic—it would be downright perverse and plainly manipulative—if a decision coherently explicable only in terms of a concern such as this were to be invoked in defense of state or local policies or programs challenged precisely on the ground that, in violation of the fourteenth amendment, they endanger those same individual rights to decent physical protection. States may not, having secured the invalidation of the challenged congressional amendments on the basis of an argument that those amendments would hinder their ability to provide services characterized as essential to their existence, then argue that their citizens have no right to such services.

If *National League of Cities* is to be read as protecting rights to certain government services, then it follows, perhaps surprisingly, that Congress could alter the result of that decision by reenacting minimum wage regulations for public employees as one possible vindication of the rights of those employees to equality, liberty, and property. For the recognition of a governmental duty to assure that basic material needs are somehow met precludes the response that minimum wage legislation is necessarily reflective only of a policy preference based on concerns with the national economy. Once we have recognized affirmative rights against government, Congress may claim that it is just such rights that it is vindicating for public employees by ensuring that they receive a minimum wage. So long as this is in fact the basis of Congress' action, it could well prove sufficient to override the claims of the state.

Thus the premises underlying the holding of *National League of Cities* paradoxically may provide the foundation for congressional rejection of the decision itself—a final refutation of the extravagant claims of state sovereignty which, encouraged more by the Court's talismanic invocations of federalism than by any analysis of the actual significance it found in the federal structure, some may wish to find in the Court's opinion. That these conclusions could surprise some of the Justices may seem odd but should not be thought decisive. For even a Court motivated to cut back on federal vindication of personal claims might structure such cutbacks in ways reflecting an inchoate recognition that those claims are propelled by a justice too insistent to be denied.

*"It is no easy matter to ... specify the distinctively 'sovereign' attributes that render states resistant to commerce-clause regulation."*

# State Sovereignty Is Not an Abstraction

### Frank I. Michelman

*Frank I. Michelman is a Robert Walmsley University Professor at Harvard Law School. In his discussion of* National League of Cities v. Usery, *Michelman analyzes William J. Brennan's impassioned dissent and attack on the majority's notion of state sovereignty, arguing that Brennan was mistaken when he claimed that such sovereignty was an abstraction with no substance. He examines Brennan's criticism and tries to understand the real meaning of states' rights and sovereignty in the decision. Michelman concludes that "sovereignty," as the Court understood it in* National League of Cities v. Usery, *stands for the state's role of providing for the interests of its citizens in receiving important social services.*

A share of the blame for what follows belongs to Mr. Justice [William] Brennan, whose twenty years of distinguished labor on behalf of our constitutional system—on behalf, I should say, of the men, women, and children whose rights and concerns that system serves—this journal [*The Yale Law Journal*] justly celebrates.

It was the Justice who, by his striking and powerful dissent in *National League of Cities v. Usery* (NLC), first made me

Frank I. Michelman, "States' Rights and States' Roles: Permutations of 'Sovereignty' in *National League of Cities v. Usery*," *The Yale Law Journal*, vol. 86, May 1977, pp. 1165–73. Copyright © 1977 The Yale Law Journal Company, Inc. Reproduced by permission of the publisher and author.

think there must be even more to that case than meets the eye. His opinion is remarkable for its depth of feeling, its sense of occasion, of foreboding, of fatal and momentous choice. The eloquence is disciplined and surgical—not so sweepingly flamboyant as, say, the impassioned [Felix] Frankfurter's, but as stirring. The opinion speaks with a controlled intensity that at first seems disconsonant with both the immediate impact of the Court's decision (denial of congressional minimum-wage protection to state and municipal employees) and its broader doctrinal significance (recognition of some state governmental immunity from congressional regulation under the commerce clause). Both developments, to be sure, are important. But it seems unlikely that the immediate impact taken by itself—if, say, it had resulted from a disputable statutory interpretation rather than from a broad affirmation of constitutionally based states' rights—can explain Justice Brennan's dramatic response. Similarly, the states' rights development, as surprising as it seems to many in light of the most immediately relevant precedents, had long been a possibility latent and unresolved in tax-immunity doctrine, and recently had been foreshadowed by Court decisions reflecting special sensitivity to a state's interest in retaining control over its internal governmental arrangements. Why, then, this most arresting protest now?

## Brennan's Attack

We can begin with Justice Brennan's attack on the Court's state-sovereignty notion as "an abstraction without substance." As will appear, I think the Justice risked some misunderstanding—perhaps even missed an important point—when he put the matter just that way. But there is enough truth in his charge to let it serve as the starting point for analysis of the sovereignty notion set forth in *NLC*. For, as we are about to find, it is no easy matter to ascribe operational content to that notion—to specify the distinctively "sovereign" attributes that render states resistant to commerce-clause regulation—so that the notion will be both internally intelligible and consistent with the totality of the *NLC* decision and its reasoning. One might intuitively think that a state's sovereignty must consist in some or all of the special *powers* it has as a legislative authority; or in the crucial *choices* it makes (through exercise of those powers) about the basic allocation and definition (or "structure") of roles and functions in society; or in the special ("political") *processes* of choice that characterize it. But each of those interpretations is ruled out by some or another aspect of the *NLC* decision itself. The only interpretation that is compatible with the decision taken as a whole, I shall argue, is a surprising one that leads in directions the Justices do not seem to have intended or anticipated.

The problem of infusing the abstraction of state sovereignty with legal substance is that of picking out those instances of congressional action that are constitutionally questionable because they impinge directly on "states." Despite the Idealist overtones in *NLC*'s references to "States as *States*," the Court plainly means "state" in the historically contingent sense of state-in-the-federal-system; not State as a philosophical absolute like Family, Corporation, or Individual. Still, we need some way of differentiating "the states" from "the people." Just about everything Congress does is intended to affect persons who in fact are citizens of states, and whose activities or property in fact are found within the borders of states; and every one of these effects is, as likely as not, discrepant in some way from what the citizenry of one or another state would have chosen for itself. Presumably only a select few of these effects will ever be regarded as impinging on "states as states."

## A Common-Sense Distinction

It might seem that there is no great mystery about how to distinguish "the states" from "the people." We know perfectly well, granting that there are intermediate hard cases, how to distinguish governmental from nongovernmental *powers* and *forms of organization*: governments are distinguished by their acknowledged, lawful authority—not dependent on property ownership—to coerce a territorially defined and imperfectly voluntary membership by acts of regulation, taxation, and condemnation, the exercise of which authority is determined by majoritarian and representative procedures. It may well be this common-sense distinction that the Court has in mind. But why so? What is it about organizations having these governmental attributes that makes them (as distinguished from all the other agencies that operate within a state under the sanction of its laws and institutions) specially needful of protection from congressional interference?

Prompted by the Court's Idealist locutions we might wonder whether the Justices had in mind something akin to a Hegelian [as in the philosophy of Georg Wilhelm Friedrich Hegel] distinction between "state" and "civil society"—where "civil society" stands for institutionalized accommodation of the interplay of particular wills and interests, and "state" represents the transcendence of those particular wills and interests in universal principles of right. But we need not wonder long. For if the essence of statehood were considered to be the generation of universal principles of right (subject, of course, to the authority of Congress within its limited sphere of competence), then the combined results of the preemption doctrine, *NLC*, and *United States v. Darby* (in which the Court upheld against a claim of states' rights the power of Congress to regulate wages in the private sector) would be just precisely wrong: congressional action in areas of disputable federal competence would be most vulnerable insofar as it displaced the state from its role of universal legislator and law-enforcer, and least vulnerable insofar as it curbed the state in its guise of active agent having particular interests opposed to other particular interests such as those of its employees.

What is it, then, that is especially significant about governmental powers and forms, if not some link between them and the role of the state as a maker and enforcer of laws? Possibly the significance of governmental powers and forms is thought by the Court to lie in their connection with certain (kinds of) welfare-related social functions. The government, then, far from being opposed to civil society, would be seen as a part of it: the people self-organized to perform functions conducive to their welfare.

But if we adopt such a welfare-oriented, functional view of the *government* as service-provider, we are again at a loss to explain why *a state's* immunity to congressional regulation should encompass only its governmental organs. For on such a view the *state* must be something that stands behind, that shapes and structures a civil society in which the *government* is but one among many agents. That state-structured civil society consists of a set of rules and practices that allocate powers, some plainly "public" or "governmental," some plainly "private" or "proprietary," some hard to classify. A state's "choice" to allocate (including its inclination to leave) powers and functions to private organs seems no less significant or purposive than its choice to create governmental responsibilities; its choice to create spheres of decentralization, or of unregulated market activity, seems no less significant or purposive than its choice to create spheres of centralization or collectivization. Neither type of choice seems any more a matter of a state's "internal affairs," or "integrity," or "structure," than the other. Indeed, neither type is intelligible except with regard to the possibility of the other, and there seems no a priori ground for treating either of the reciprocally defining possibilities as primary. "Structure" seems to be just the totality of the choices. If so, *Darby* countenances a congressional impingement on the structural affairs of states no less momentous than the one averted in *NLC*.

## Governments and Provision of Services

We have seen, then, that a state's "sovereignty," as conceived in *NLC*, can consist neither in a notion of the state as the object of political loyalty and legitimate arbiter of rights, nor in a notion of the state as the embodiment of political choice about the basic "structuring" of roles and functions in civil society. That neither of those was in fact the Court's notion is strongly confirmed by its decision to include municipal governments under the state's protective "sovereignty" mantle. That this decision was a focused and deliberate one is clear on the face of the opinion. That it was by no means an inevitable one is clear from the established doctrine *denying* municipalities immunity from suit in federal tribunals, which "states" enjoy under the Eleventh Amendment. The *NLC* opinion offers no reason for protecting municipalities, along with states, from congressional regulation under the commerce clause, beyond noting that municipalities "derive their authority and power from their respective States." But that, we have already noted, is no less true of private corporations (or of individuals in their capacities as property owners) fully exposed to congressional regulatory authority. Whatever else might distinguish municipalities from those private entities, it plainly cannot be any attribution to municipalities of a law-giving, rights-declaring, or "structuring" role resembling that of the state itself. A crucial passage in the Court's opinion strongly implies that the special solicitude for municipalities arises out of quite different concerns. The Court says that extension of the minimum wage to local governments will

> significantly alter or displace the States' abilities to structure employer-employee relationships in such areas as fire prevention, police protection, sanitation, public health, and parks and recreation. These activities are typical of those performed by state and local governments in discharging their dual functions of administering the public law and furnishing public services. Indeed, it is functions such as

these which governments are created to provide, services such as these which the States have traditionally afforded their citizens. If Congress may withdraw from the States the authority to make those fundamental employment decisions upon which their systems for performance of these functions must rest, we think there would be little left of the States' "'separate and independent existence.'"

So it seems that what is "sovereign" about municipalities is not their *legislative* position or significance, but the states' customary reliance on them to provide for the interest of citizens in receiving certain important social services.

## Sovereignty's Protections

But perhaps this conclusion is too hasty. Perhaps sovereignty inheres in the special value or sanctity ascribed to *processes* of political choice as such (or of modes of community interaction that such processes are believed to foster or contain), so that special justification is required for congressional action that would directly contradict the results of such processes, or restrict the occasions for resorting to them, or curtail their effective scope. We have already noted, however, that congressional power can quite drastically impair the state's own political competence when directed to a state's private sector. And besides, congressional action is *itself* a constitutionally sanctified political process, and the general idea of a dual federalism seems to offer no firm ground for preferring the "integrity" of state and local politics to that of national politics.

Or does it? Can we perhaps read the Great Compromise as protecting the vitality of political processes at *both* levels by the somewhat arbitrary device of granting to Congress broad authority over the states' private sectors while sharply limiting its authority over state and local public sectors—thereby ensuring that a state can always preserve breathing space for its political life by absorbing activities into its political sphere, its governmental sector? On this view, the special harm threatened by the Fair Labor Standards Act (FLSA) amendments would be just the constricting pressure they exert on the fiscally feasible size and range of a state's (and its municipalities') governmental undertakings, [and] possible resultant impoverishment of political interaction at the state and local levels.

Even this last-ditch effort to connect the *NLC* decision with a strictly political notion of "sovereignty" is defeated by the decision itself—specifically by its refusal to extend the protective mantle of sovereignty to "areas that the States have not regarded as integral parts of their governmental activities," such as operating a railroad. While the Court's opinion uses the word "integral" in at least five places to differentiate protected from unprotected state activities or "functions," at no point does it undertake to give content to this vague locution. From the opinion as a whole one can fairly gather that "integral" has roughly the same meaning as "typical" or "traditional." But that reading means that a state's "sovereignty"—its special virtue that evokes the protection of the *NLC* doctrine—cannot be its embodiment of processes of political choice valued as such. For under such a sanctity-of-politics view of state sovereignty, a state's (or locality's) political choice to extend the range of its public involvements into some nontypical or nontraditional area would apparently be a quintessential instance of that very political vitality that the Constitution supposedly meant to nurture and protect.

I think we are finally forced to the conclusion that in holding that the FLSA amendments (especially as applied to municipalities) impinged upon state sovereignty, the Court in *NLC* was using "sovereignty" to stand—rather unexpectedly— for nothing more nor less than the state's role of providing for the interests of its citizens in receiving important social services. It is only this unusual and extremely specialized sense of "sovereignty" that allows the Court to say, with even a semblance of plausibility, that states are acting peculiarly "in their capacities as sovereign governments" when they empower municipal governments to contract with their own employees or that Congress by extending the minimum wage law to state and, especially, local governments "has sought to wield its power in a fashion that would impair the States' 'ability to function effectively . . . [within]' the federal system of government embodied in the Constitution."

> *"The harsh reaction to* Usery *is one aspect of a widespread pattern that inverts the priorities of the framers: an obsessive concern for using the Constitution to protect individuals' rights."*

# Individuals' Rights Do Not Override the Structural Principle of Federalism

*Robert F. Nagel*

*Robert F. Nagel is the Ira C. Rothgerber Jr. Professor of Constitutional Law at the University of Colorado Law School. In the following viewpoint, he discusses the negative reaction by prominent legal scholars to the decision in* National League of Cities v. Usery. *The Court in that case found that Congress was acting unconstitutionally in regulating the working conditions (wages, overtime, labor standards) of public employees of the states. Nagel asserts that scholars' lack of understanding has to do less with the decision itself than with the modern obsession with using the Constitution to protect individual rights. He believes the framers of the Constitution were more concerned with protecting underlying judicial principles and constitutional structure.*

After almost forty years of sanctioning the growth of the congressional power to regulate commerce, the Supreme Court in *National League of Cities v. Usery* held that the extension of the wage and hour provisions of the Fair Labor Standards Act to most state employees was unconstitutional as a

Robert F. Nagel, "Federalism as a Fundamental Value: *National League of Cities* in Perspective," *Supreme Court Review*, 1981, pp. 81–109. Copyright © 1981 University of Chicago Press. All rights reserved. Reproduced by permission.

violation of the principle of federalism. Although some serious commentary had suggested that the Court's record prior to *Usery* verged on abdication of constitutional responsibilities, *Usery* precipitated criticism that was extraordinary both for its breadth and severity. Justice [William] Brennan, a respected and unapologetic practitioner of judicial power and imaginative constitutional analysis when the issues involve individuals' rights, labeled the decision "an abstraction without substance" and a "patent usurpation." Three prominent scholars reacted to the decision extremely critically. Professors [Laurence] Tribe and [Frank] Michelman, both resourceful at constitutional interpretation, professed themselves totally unable to understand the explanation offered by the Court in *Usery* and proposed that the decision could make sense only as an inchoate statement of a right to the provision of certain state services. Professor [Jesse] Choper reacted with a forceful argument that, even if *Usery* were constitutionally correct on the merits, the Court should have held such matters to be nonjusticiable in order to save its resources for—that phrase again—the protection of individual rights. Many others also criticized *Usery*, and those who were at all supportive of the decision were muted or ambivalent.

## Obsession with Individual Rights

The harsh reaction to *Usery* is one aspect of a widespread pattern that inverts the priorities of the framers: an obsessive concern for using the Constitution to protect individuals' rights. This fascination with rights reinforces a form of instrumentalism that is too confining to be an adequate way to think about constitutional law. If *Usery* is viewed without these intellectual constraints, a rather plain and defensible explanation for the decision emerges. My major purpose [in this essay] is not to insist that *Usery* was ultimately "correct," but to suggest that the inability to understand *Usery* demonstrates the extent to which the capacity to appreciate some important constitutional principles is being lost.

Judicial decisions generally reflect a priority in favor of protecting individuals' rights over the structural principles of separation of powers and federalism. Decisions directly resting on these structural principles are rare compared with decisions involving individual rights. Issues of federalism and separation of powers are usually analyzed in terms of nonconstitutional doctrines. For example, they are frequently reduced to matters of statutory construction. The scope of the judicial power over states is often discussed in amorphous, discretionary terms—such as equitable discretion, standing, justiciability, and comity. Even when structural principles are treated as fully constitutional matters, their main influence is on the definition of individual rights. Those decisions that do deal unambiguously with structural values for their own sake demonstrate less explanatory creativity than do decisions dealing with rights, a fact that suggests a relative lack of judicial interest in structural matters if not lower quality opinions. Missing from decisions involving structural values is any use of the doctrinal innovations used so often in decisions involving rights. There are no analyses of motive, no dissections of legislative purpose, no demands that less drastic means be used, no tiers of judicial scrutiny. Instead, decisions having to do with structure frequently rest on the baldest forms of "balancing" and on undeveloped references to such generalities as "undue impairment" of the states' functions. Finally, cases in which rights are articulated are frequently followed by a series of decisions that are designed to "actualize" the original right, and in the process the right is often recast in even more ambitious terms. Important cases that articulate structural values tend quickly to be limited and then largely abandoned.

Modern judges work diligently at redesigning local educational programs and at defining the acceptable number of square feet in a prison cell. They void a multiplicity of laws relating to hair length, sexual preference, and abortion. But they deal rarely and, for the most part, gingerly with the great issues of power distribution that were faced so ambitiously and successfully by the framers.

Academic writing generally reflects the same priority. Scholarly discussion of constitutional structure often falls back on the more familiar issues of individual rights. For example, Professor [Charles Lund] Black's *Structure and Relationship in Constitutional Law* illuminates the possibilities of argument based on structure only to apply quickly that potential to the definition of individual rights. Professor [John] Ely's *Democracy and Distrust* emphasizes the central importance of democratic self-government in the constitutional design, but this insight is enlisted chiefly in support of rationalizing the [Earl] Warren Court's creative definition of individual rights. (The book is then criticized, not for overemphasizing the dependence of democratic processes on individual rights, but for attempting to define rights by reference to considerations other than the needs of individuals.) Many books and articles appear on the injunctive devices that lower federal courts are using against states in an effort to implement individuals' constitutional rights. Much of this commentary seeks to conceptualize individuals' rights and the judicial function in ways that permit significant aspects of self-government to be assumed by the courts for the sake of remaking the world to suit some ideal suggested by values implicit in certain rights. Much of the rest of the commentary emphasizes the practicalities of judicial enforcement and largely assumes that, if courts are able to implement individual rights effectively, implementation must have priority over other values. Those that examine the remedial role of the federal courts as an aspect of constitutional structure are quickly urged to return to the proper business of legal scholars, which is expressly defined as arguing about rights.

Scholarly preoccupation with rights is also evident in the tolerant and highly imaginative approaches frequently taken in the definition of rights. Scholars commonly argue that it ought to be no bar to a constitutional claim that there is ambiguity about whether the framers intended a certain interpretation or that they did not consider a possible interpretation of a constitutional right. The argument is extended in such important areas as school desegregation to include definitions of rights that are rather clearly in conflict with historical intent. It is not uncommon for sophisticated scholars to make unembarrassed arguments for an interpretation of a right based largely on the personal values of the proponent of the right. What more than this can be meant by assertions about "goodness" or "minimal standards of human dignity" or "personhood"? Such argumentation, even if it involves more than private values, demonstrates how wide and free the scope of acceptable constitutional argument about rights is. Indeed, scholarship indulges almost any amount of philosophical or psychological vagueness and complexity when the goal is defining rights. We ponder how "just wants" or the "mediation of liberal conversation" or "equal respect and concern" or the ideas of [political philosopher] Roberto Unger might bear on the definition of rights.

In contrast, scholars often exhibit a kind of intellectual crabbedness when structural claims are made. Consider the scholars who were content to rest a defense of expanded institutional rights on an assertion about "fostering minimal standards of dignity." They had just tested federalism and separation of power claims about institutional injunctions by demanding to see evidence that the framers actually foresaw and opposed judicial operation of public institutions. Almost any slight ambiguity about historical intent is urged to help defeat structural claims. Similarly, arguments based on concepts such as separation of powers or democratic accountability are termed hopelessly indeterminate. The same scholar who demands specificity in the concept of "state sovereignty" would ground interpretations of individual rights on values such as "a meaningful opportunity [for individuals] to realize their humanity."

## Undervaluing Protection of Principles

In short, the hostile reaction to *Usery* is part of a broader pattern: Many jurists and scholars tend to envision constitutional values mainly in terms of individuals' rights and to undervalue judicial protection of principles that allocate decision-making responsibility among governmental units. This tendency may be largely a consequence of the influence of the lawsuit in shaping views of the Constitution. Lawsuits, of course, are discrete arguments, usually involving an individual, and they are often resolved by labeling the interests of one side as "rights"; thus, the lawsuit itself tends to convert even organizational matters into individual concerns. But to see the purposes of judicial review almost entirely in terms of securing individual rights is to invert the priorities of the framers and ultimately to trivialize the Constitution. The framers' political theory was immediately concerned with organization, not individuals. Their most important contributions had to do with principles of power allocation—with the blending and separation of power among the branches of government and with the bold effort to create a strong national government while maintaining strong state governments. This structure itself was to be the great protection of the individual, not the "parchment barriers" that were later (and with modest expectations) added to the document. Even the danger of local majoritarian excess—so frequently cited today as a justification for vigorous protection of individual rights—cannot reconcile the modern emphasis on rights with the priorities of the framers. Although aware of the threat posed by "faction," the Federalists proposed social heterogeneity and layered government as the protection, not the Bill of Rights, which, after all, was originally thought to restrain only the national government.

The modern priority on individuals' rights is striking in light of the common assumption that judicial review allows for some continuity in the articulation of our most basic principles. In adopting a viewpoint and a vocabulary that focuses on individuals, modern judges and scholars have tended to shut themselves off from full participation in the great debates about governmental theory begun by the framers. The writings of Professor Choper, the bluntest and most extreme critic of judicial enforcement of structural values, provide a more specific understanding of how this participation has been limited. . . .

## Protecting Constitutional Structure

The Court in *Usery* displayed a sure feel for protecting the "essential role of the States in our federal system of government" as the framers defined that role. Despite the Court's failure to refer specifically to the role of the states as political competitors to the national government, the tracking of the Federalists' theory was not coincidental. The case law that informed and shaped the Court's assumptions about federalism was no doubt influenced by the framers' ideas, and, in any event, the *Usery* Court, like the framers, focused on what is necessary for the states' "separate and independent existence."

*Usery*, then, was not incomprehensible to its critics because its holding and explanation were unrelated to the Constitution. It was incomprehensible because of the critics' intellectual habits which had developed out of long concern for questions of individuals' rights.

Decisions like *Usery* that protect constitutional structure are different from the more familiar efforts of courts to protect rights. Structural principles such as federalism are intended to maintain a rough system of power allocation over long periods of time. There is no analogy to the adjudication of rights where, at some point in time, desegregation must be achieved or enough services must be provided. Structure is a process that is maintained, not achieved. The courts' function in matters of structure is largely to sustain (or at least not undercut) the understandings, the attitudes, and the emotional ties that underlie the system of power allocation. These objectives may be intangible, but they are directly relevant to preserving the constitutional system, since that system presupposes divided loyalties and complex attitudes toward authority. Structural decisions are not necessarily based on the injustice of depriving a single individual of a particular allocation of authority. Hence, the assertion of structural values is not essential in every case where they are potentially implicated; nevertheless, their assertion in especially appropriate cases like *Usery* is important because of the indirect, long-run consequences to the whole political system of ignoring the underpinnings of constitutional structure. These consequences are not adequately described by images of states as "empty vessels" or "gutted shells." Such metaphors are more expressive of the critics' urge to render the issues tangible (and therefore more familiar) than of the values at stake in a dispute about federalism. In the Federalists' scheme, the states were to be maintained partly for their own sakes and partly as a tool for assuring adequate levels of political responsiveness, competition, and participation.

Much of the scholarly and judicial attention to the definition of individual rights is aimed at achieving these same goals by more direct means. Definitions of free speech, equal protection, procedural due process, privacy, and other rights are grounded on the belief that such protections will produce the kind of independent individuals who can participate vigorously in the political process. And it may be that these rights are ultimately important to the potential for self-government. But, quite aside from the familiar charge that enforcement of such rights centralizes too much power at the national level, excessive attention to rights can be a threat to self-government. A subtle conflict exists between rights, taken too seriously, and structure. The frame of mind that is created by concentration on the direct, tangible protection of individuals does not easily appreciate the less determinate requirements of constitutional structure. A judicial system deeply engaged in achieving immediate justice for all individuals will not be sensitive to, or much interested in, the intellectual and emotional preconditions for political competition between sovereigns. The "constitutional law" that develops in such a system will be more attuned to the demands of measurement and the excitement of accomplishment than to the full range of the framers' concerns.

Suppose for a moment that divided and limited loyalties are not as important as the right to contraceptives for preserving the capacity for self-government in the modern world. At least, a decision like *Usery* that presumed there might be some small usefulness in promoting the framers' organizational theory ought not to have been dismissed as *constitutionally* incomprehensible. That the decision was so widely unappreciated ought to be unsettling to anyone who is not certain that the framers' structural principles are worthless today.

CHAPTER 4

# Federalizing the
# Minimum Wage

# Case Overview

## *Garcia v. San Antonio Metropolitan Transit Authority* (1985)

In *National League of Cities v. Usery* (1974), the Supreme Court ruled that the wage and hour provisions of the 1938 Fair Labor Standards Act (FLSA) could not be applied against states "in areas of traditional governmental functions," such as public schools and hospitals and mass transit agencies. In 1979, however, the Department of Labor issued an opinion that San Antonio's mass transit agency was "not constitutionally immune from the application of the FLSA," and thus was required to pay overtime wages. Two months later the San Antonio Metropolitan Transit Authority (SAMTA) filed an action against the Department of Labor. On that same day, Joe G. Garcia and several other SAMTA workers sued their employer for overtime pay.

The question brought before the Supreme Court in *Garcia v. San Antonio Metropolitan Transit Authority* (1985) was whether "municipal ownership and operation of a mass transit system is a traditional governmental function" and is thus exempt from the overtime requirements of the FLSA. The U.S. Supreme Court ruled in favor of the municipality and overturned a decision it had made nine years earlier in *National League of Cities v. Usery*.

Justice Harry Blackmun's reversal resulted primarily from what he saw as the Court's inability to draw a consistent line between congressional regulations that interfered excessively with state sovereignty and those that did not. The Court had, indeed, set out criteria for making the judgment in *National League of Cities*. This case arose, however, because the criteria (namely, the "traditional government function" test) were vague. After noting the inconsistency of decisions the Court had made on the basis of those guidelines, Blackmun concluded that "the attempt to draw the boundaries of state regulatory immunity in terms of 'traditional governmental function' is not only unworkable but is also inconsistent with established principles of federalism." This did not mean he thought states' interests no longer needed protection from federal intrusion. What he rejected was a certain method for accomplishing that goal. In particular, Blackmun rejected the strategy of relying so heavily on the courts to decide whether particular pieces of legislation violated state sovereignty. Blackmun argued that "the structure of the Federal Government itself was relied on to insulate the interests of the states." Specifically, Blackmun pointed to the protections created by state representation in the Senate.

Four justices dissented from the majority. Justice Lewis F. Powell Jr. in his response argued that *Garcia* was not strong enough to overturn all the prior decisions based on *National League of Cities*. Also, he noted, all legislation contains nebulous language and it is the job of the Court to clarify such laws and to guide their application. The majority, Powell concluded, acted irresponsibly in refusing to do so. Finally, Powell argued that the authors of the Constitution intended for the Court to function as a check on congressional power. Blackmun's refusal to engage had the effect of disabling an important safeguard and balancing mechanism. Justice William Rehnquist in his dissent predicted that *Garcia* would not stand and that *National League of Cities* "will . . . in time command the support of a majority of this Court."

The Court's decision in *Garcia* served to weaken state and Tenth Amendment rights and reflected a broader interpretation of Congress's power to regulate interstate commerce as granted under the Constitution's commerce clause. The pendulum inched back toward the states in later cases (*New York v. United States* [1992] and *United States v. Lopez* [1995]).

Though the Court did not overturn *Garcia*, it did reassert its power to set limits on Congress's power to regulate interstate commerce.

"Nothing in the overtime and minimum wage requirements of the [Fair Labor Standards Act] . . . is destructive of state sovereignty."

# Majority Opinion: State Employers Are Bound by Federal Legislation

## Harry Blackmun

*Harry Blackmun, an associate justice of the Supreme Court from 1970 to 1994, is best known as the author of the majority opinion in the 1973* Roe v. Wade *decision, overturning laws restricting abortion. He also wrote and delivered the five-to-four majority opinion in the case of* Garcia v. San Antonio Metropolitan Transit Authority *(1985), which ruled that the overtime and minimum wage provisions of the Fair Labor Standards Act (FLSA) did not violate the Constitution's commerce clause, thus overturning* National League of Cities v. Usery *(1976). In its 1976 decision, the Court had held that the application of such wage and hour provisions to state or local employees "in areas of traditional government functions" was unconstitutional. In* Garcia v. San Antonio Metropolitan Transit Authority, *Blackmum argued that the lower court decisions following* National League of Cities *had failed to establish any sound principle for determining which government operations were "traditional" and essential to state sovereignty, and thus immune from impairment by congressional regulations. He rejects as well the notion expressed in* National League of Cities *that the Constitution's rec-*

Harry Blackmun, majority opinion, *Garcia v. San Antonio Metropolitan Transit Authority*, U.S. Supreme Court, 1985.

*ognition of state sovereignty implies limits on the power of the federal government to regulate the labor practices of the states.*

We revisit in these cases an issue raised in *National League of Cities v. Usery* (1976). In that litigation, this Court, by a sharply divided vote, ruled that the Commerce Clause does not empower Congress to enforce the minimum wage and overtime provisions of the Fair Labor Standards Act (FLSA) against the States "in areas of traditional governmental functions." Although *National League of Cities* supplied some examples of "traditional governmental functions," it did not offer a general explanation of how a "traditional" function is to be distinguished from a "nontraditional" one. Since then, federal and state courts have struggled with the task, thus imposed, of identifying a traditional function for purposes of state immunity under the Commerce Clause.

In the present cases, a Federal District Court concluded that municipal ownership and operation of a mass transit system is a traditional governmental function and thus, under *National League of Cities*, is exempt from the obligations imposed by the FLSA. Faced with the identical question, three Federal Courts of Appeals and one state appellate court have reached the opposite conclusion.

Our examination of this "function" standard applied in these and other cases over the last eight years now persuades us that the attempt to draw the boundaries of state regulatory immunity in terms of "traditional governmental function" is not only unworkable but is also inconsistent with established principles of federalism and, indeed, with those very federalism principles on which *National League of Cities* purported to rest. That case, accordingly, is overruled. . . .

## Little Headway Made

Thus far, this Court itself has made little headway in defining the scope of the governmental functions deemed protected under *National League of Cities*. In that case, the Court set forth examples of protected and unprotected functions, but provided no explanation of how those examples were identified. The only other case in which the Court has had occasion to address the problem is *Long Island* [*United Transportation Union v. Long Island Rail Road Co.* (1982)]. We there observed:

> The determination of whether a federal law impairs a state's authority with respect to "areas of traditional [state] functions" may at times be a difficult one.

The accuracy of that statement is demonstrated by this Court's own difficulties in *Long Island* in developing a workable standard for "traditional governmental functions." We relied in large part there on "the *historical reality* that the operation of railroads is not among the functions *traditionally* performed by state and local governments," but we simultaneously disavowed "a static historical view of state functions generally immune from federal regulation." We held that the inquiry into a particular function's "traditional" nature was merely a means of determining whether the federal statute at issue unduly handicaps "basic state prerogatives," but we did not offer an explanation of what makes one state function a "basic prerogative" and another function not basic. Finally, having disclaimed a rigid reliance on the historical pedigree of state involvement in a particular area, we nonetheless found it appropriate to emphasize the extended historical record of *federal* involvement in the field of rail transportation.

Many constitutional standards involve "undoubte[d] . . . gray areas," *Fry v. United States* (1975) (dissenting opinion), and, despite the difficulties that this Court and other courts have encountered so far, it normally might be fair to venture the assumption that case-by-case development would lead to a workable standard for determining whether a particular governmental function should be immune from federal regulation under the Commerce Clause. . . .

## "Integral" and "Traditional" Functions

We believe, however, that there is a more fundamental problem at work here, a problem that explains why the Court was never able to provide a basis for the governmental/proprietary distinction in the intergovernmental tax immunity cases and why an attempt to draw similar distinctions with respect to federal regulatory authority under *National League of Cities* is unlikely to succeed regardless of how the distinctions are phrased. The problem is that neither the governmental/proprietary distinction nor any other that purports to separate out important governmental functions can be faithful to the role of federalism in a democratic society. The essence of our federal system is that, within the realm of authority left open to them under the Constitution, the States must be equally free to engage in any activity that their citizens choose for the common weal, no matter how unorthodox or unnecessary anyone else—including the judiciary—deems state involvement to be. Any rule of state immunity that looks to the "traditional," "integral," or "necessary" nature of governmental functions inevitably invites an unelected federal judiciary to make decisions about which state policies it favors and which ones it dislikes. . . .

We therefore now reject, as unsound in principle and unworkable in practice, a rule of state immunity from federal regulation that turns on a judicial appraisal of whether a particular governmental function is "integral" or "traditional." Any such rule leads to inconsistent results at the same time that it disserves principles of democratic self-governance, and it breeds inconsistency precisely because it is divorced from those principles. If there are to be limits on the Federal Government's power to interfere with state functions—as undoubtedly there are—we must look elsewhere to find them. We accordingly return to the underlying issue that confronted this Court in *National League of Cities*—the manner in which the Constitution insulates States from the reach of Congress' power under the Commerce Clause.

## Limitations on the Commerce Clause

The central theme of *National League of Cities* was that the States occupy a special position in our constitutional system, and that the scope of Congress' authority under the Commerce Clause must reflect that position. Of course, the Commerce Clause, by its specific language, does not provide any special limitation on Congress' actions with respect to the States. *See EEOC v. Wyoming* (1983) (concurring opinion). It is equally true, however, that the text of the Constitution provides the beginning, rather than the final answer, to every inquiry into questions of federalism, for "[b]ehind the words of the constitutional provisions are postulates which limit and control." *Monaco v. Mississippi* (1934). *National League of Cities* reflected the general conviction that the Constitution precludes "the National Government [from] devour[ing] the essentials of state sovereignty." *Maryland v. Wirtz* (dissenting opinion). In order to be faithful to the underlying federal premises of the Constitution, courts must look for the "postulates which limit and control."

What has proved problematic is not the perception that the Constitution's federal structure imposes limitations on the Commerce Clause, but rather the nature and content of those limitations. One approach to defining the limits on Congress' authority to regulate the States under the Commerce Clause is to identify certain underlying elements of political sovereignty that are deemed essential to the States' "separate and independent existence." *Lane County v. Oregon*, 7 Wall. (1869). This approach obviously underlay the Court's use of the "traditional governmental function" concept in *National League of Cities*. It also has led to the separate requirement that the challenged federal statute "address matters that are indisputably 'attribute[s] of state sovereignty.'" In *National League of Cities* itself, for example, the Court concluded that decisions by a State concerning the wages and hours of its employees are an "undoubted attribute of state sovereignty." The opinion did not explain what aspects of such decisions made them such an "undoubted attribute," and the Court since then has remarked on the uncertain scope of the concept. The point of the inquiry, however, has remained to single out particular features of a State's internal governance that are deemed to be intrinsic parts of state sovereignty. We doubt that courts ultimately can identify principled constitutional limitations on the scope of Congress' Commerce Clause powers over the States merely by relying on *a priori* definitions of state sovereignty. In part, this is because of the elusiveness of objective criteria for "fundamental" elements of state sovereignty, a problem we have witnessed in the search for "traditional governmental functions." There is, however, a more fundamental reason: the sovereignty of the States is limited by the Constitution itself. A variety of sovereign powers, for example, are withdrawn from the States by Article I, § 10. Section 8 of the same Article works an equally sharp contraction of state sovereignty by authorizing Congress to exercise a wide range of legislative powers and (in conjunction with the Supremacy Clause of Article VI) to displace contrary state legislation. By providing for final review of questions of federal law in this Court, Article III curtails the sovereign power of the States' judiciaries to make authoritative determinations of law. *See Martin v. Hunter's Lessee.* Finally, the developed application, through the Fourteenth Amendment, of the greater part of the Bill of Rights to the States limits the sovereign authority that States otherwise would possess to legislate with respect to their citizens and to conduct their own affairs. . . .

## Views of State Sovereignty

When we look for the States' "residuary and inviolable sovereignty," in the shape of the constitutional scheme, rather than in predetermined notions of sovereign power, a different measure of state sovereignty emerges. Apart from the limitation on federal authority inherent in the delegated nature of Congress' Article I powers, the principal means chosen by the Framers to ensure the role of the States in the federal system lies in the structure of the Federal Government itself. It is no novelty to observe that the composition of the Federal Government was designed in large part to protect the States from overreaching by Congress. The Framers thus gave the States a role in the selection both of the Executive and the Legislative Branches of the Federal Government. The States were vested with indirect influence over the House of Representatives and the Presidency by their control of electoral qualifications and their role in Presidential elections. They were given more direct influence in the Senate, where each State received equal representation and each Senator was to be selected by the legislature of his State. The significance attached to the States' equal representation in the Senate is underscored by the prohibition of any constitutional amendment divesting a State of equal representation without the State's consent.

The extent to which the structure of the Federal Government itself was relied on to insulate the interests of the States is evident in the views of the Framers. James Madison explained that the Federal Government

> will partake sufficiently of the spirit [of the States], to be disinclined to invade the rights of the individual States, or the prerogatives of their governments. . . .

The effectiveness of the federal political process in preserving the States' interests is apparent even today in the course of federal legislation. On the one hand, the States have been able to direct a substantial proportion of federal revenues into their own treasuries in the form of general and program-specific grants in aid. The federal role in assisting state and local governments is a longstanding one; Congress provided federal land grants to finance state governments from the beginning of the Republic, and direct cash grants were awarded as early as 1887 under the Hatch Act. In the past quarter century alone, federal grants to States and localities have grown from $7 billion to $96 billion. As a result, federal grants now account for about one-fifth of state and local government expenditures. The States have obtained federal funding for such services as police and fire protection, education, public health and hospitals, parks and recreation, and sanitation. Moreover, at the same time that the States have exercised their influence to obtain federal support, they have been able to exempt themselves from a wide variety of obligations imposed by Congress under the Commerce Clause. For example, the Federal Power Act, the National Labor Relations Act, the Labor-Management Reporting and Disclosure Act, the Occupational Safety and Health Act, the Employee Retirement Income Security Act, and the Sherman Act all contain express or implied exemptions for States and their subdivisions. The fact that some federal statutes such as the FLSA extend general obligations to the States cannot obscure the extent to which the political position of the States in the federal system has served to minimize the burdens that the States bear under the Commerce Clause.

## Changes in Federal Government Structure

We realize that changes in the structure of the Federal Government have taken place since 1789, not the least of which has been the substitution of popular election of Senators by the adoption of the Seventeenth Amendment in 1913, and that these changes may work to alter the influence of the States in the federal political process. Nonetheless, against this background, we are convinced that the fundamental limitation that the constitutional scheme imposes on the Commerce Clause to protect the "States as States" is one of process, rather than one of result. Any substantive restraint on the exercise of Commerce Clause powers must find its justification in the procedural nature of this basic limitation, and it must be tailored to compensate for possible failings in the national political process, rather than to dictate a "sacred province of state autonomy."

Insofar as the present cases are concerned, then, we need go no further than to state that we perceive nothing in the overtime and minimum wage requirements of the FLSA, as applied to SAMTA, that is destructive of state sovereignty or violative of any constitutional provision. SAMTA faces nothing more than the same minimum wage and overtime obligations that hundreds of thousands of other employers, public as well as private, have to meet. . . .

Of course, we continue to recognize that the States occupy a special and specific position in our constitutional system, and that the scope of Congress' authority under the Commerce Clause must reflect that position. But the principal and basic limit on the federal commerce power is that inherent in all congressional action—the built-in restraints that our system provides through state participation in federal governmental action. The political process ensures that laws that unduly burden the States will not be promulgated. In the factual setting of these cases, the internal safeguards of the political process have performed as intended. . . .

Though the separate concurrence providing the fifth vote in *National League of Cities* was "not untroubled by certain possible implications" of the decision, the Court in that case attempted to articulate affirmative limits on the Commerce Clause power in terms of core governmental functions and fundamental attributes of state sovereignty. But the model of democratic decisionmaking the Court there identified underestimated, in our view, the solicitude of the national political process for the continued vitality of the States. Attempts by other courts since then to draw guidance from this model have proved it both impracticable and doctrinally barren. In sum, in *National League of Cities*, the Court tried to repair what did not need repair.

We do not lightly overrule recent precedent. We have not hesitated, however, when it has become apparent that a prior decision has departed from a proper understanding of congressional power under the Commerce Clause. Due respect for the reach of congressional power within the federal system mandates that we do so now.

*National League of Cities v. Usery* (1976) is overruled. The judgment of the District Court is reversed, and these cases are remanded to that court for further proceedings consistent with this opinion.

| *"The Court today propounds a view of federalism that pays only lipservice to the role of the States."*

# Dissenting Opinion: The Court Has Abandoned Federalism

*Lewis F. Powell Jr.*

*Lewis F. Powell Jr., nominated to the Supreme Court by Richard Nixon, was an associate justice from 1972 to 1987. In his dissent in* Garcia v. San Antonio Metropolitan Transit Authority *(1985), he argues that the majority's decision abandoned the federalism envisioned by the Framers of the Constitution and was putting states at the mercy of a centralized federal government.* Garcia *overruled* National League of Cities v. Usery *(1976), which found that Congress overstepped its bounds by seeking to regulate the labor practices of state and municipal governments. Powell laments that the notion of precedent seems to have been abandoned, saying that the* National League of Cities *decision had been "reiterated consistently over the past eight years" and should not now be invalidated. Regulations by Congress and its increasingly broad power, he charges, displace states' sovereign functions.*

The Court today, in its 5-4 decision, overrules *National League of Cities v. Usery* (1976), a case in which we held that Congress lacked authority to impose the requirements of the Fair Labor Standards Act [FLSA] on state and local gov-

Lewis F. Powell Jr., dissenting opinion, *Garcia v. San Antonio Metropolitan Transit Authority*, U.S. Supreme Court, 1985.

ernments. Because I believe this decision substantially alters the federal system embodied in the Constitution, I dissent.

There are, of course, numerous examples over the history of this Court in which prior decisions have been reconsidered and overruled. There have been few cases, however, in which the principle of *stare decisis* [precedent] and the rationale of recent decisions were ignored as abruptly as we now witness. The reasoning of the Court in *National League of Cities*, and the principle applied there, have been reiterated consistently over the past eight years. . . .

## Abandoning Precedent

Whatever effect the Court's decision may have in weakening the application of *stare decisis*, it is likely to be less important than what the Court has done to the Constitution itself. A unique feature of the United States is the federal system of government guaranteed by the Constitution and implicit in the very name of our country. Despite some genuflecting in the Court's opinion to the concept of federalism, today's decision effectively reduces the Tenth Amendment to meaningless rhetoric when Congress acts pursuant to the Commerce Clause. . . .

To leave no doubt about its intention, the Court renounces its decision in *National League of Cities* because it

> inevitably invites an unelected federal judiciary to make decisions about which state policies its favors and which ones it dislikes.

In other words, the extent to which the States may exercise their authority, when Congress purports to act under the Commerce Clause, henceforth is to be determined from time to time by political decisions made by members of the Federal Government, decisions the Court says will not be subject to judicial review. I note that it does not seem to have occurred to the Court that *it*—an unelected majority of five Justices—

today rejects almost 200 years of the understanding of the constitutional status of federalism. In doing so, there is only a single passing reference to the Tenth Amendment. Nor is so much as a dictum of any court cited in support of the view that the role of the States in the federal system may depend upon. The grace of elected federal officials, rather than on the Constitution as interpreted by this Court. . . .

## State's Sovereignty Under Attack

The Court finds that the test of state immunity approved in *National League of Cities* and its progeny is unworkable and unsound in principle. In finding the test to be unworkable, the Court begins by mischaracterizing *National League of Cities* and subsequent cases. In concluding that efforts to define state immunity are unsound in principle, the Court radically departs from long-settled constitutional values and ignores the role of judicial review in our system of government. . . .

Today's opinion does not explain how the States' role in the electoral process guarantees that particular exercises of the Commerce Clause power will not infringe on residual state sovereignty. Members of Congress are elected from the various States, but once in office, they are Members of the Federal Government. Although the States participate in the Electoral College, this is hardly a reason to view the President as a representative of the States' interest against federal encroachment. We noted recently "[t]he hydraulic pressure inherent within each of the separate Branches to exceed the outer limits of its power. . . ." The Court offers no reason to think that this pressure will not operate when Congress seeks to invoke its powers under the Commerce Clause, notwithstanding the electoral role of the States.

The Court apparently thinks that the States' success at obtaining federal funds for various projects and exemptions from the obligations of some federal statutes is indicative of the "effectiveness of the federal political process in preserving the States' interests. . . ." But such political success is not relevant to the question whether the political *processes* are the proper means of enforcing constitutional limitations. The fact that Congress generally does not transgress constitutional limits on its power to reach state activities does not make judicial review any less necessary to rectify the cases in which it does do so. The States' role in our system of government is a matter of constitutional law, not of legislative grace.

> The powers not delegated to the United States by the Constitution, nor prohibited by it to the States, are reserved to the States, respectively, or to the people.

More troubling than the logical infirmities in the Court's reasoning is the result of its holding, *i.e.*, that federal political officials, invoking the Commerce Clause, are the sole judges of the limits of their own power. This result is inconsistent with the fundamental principles of our constitutional system. At least since *Marbury v. Madison* (1803), it has been the settled province of the federal judiciary "to say what the law is" with respect to the constitutionality of Acts of Congress. In rejecting the role of the judiciary in protecting the States from federal overreaching, the Court's opinion offers no explanation for ignoring the teaching of the most famous case in our history. . . .

## The Tenth Amendment and State Powers

In contrast, the Court today propounds a view of federalism that pays only lipservice to the role of the States. Although it says that the States "unquestionably do 'retai[n] a significant measure of sovereign authority,'" it fails to recognize the broad, yet specific areas of sovereignty that the Framers intended the States to retain. Indeed, the Court barely acknowledges that the Tenth Amendment exists. That Amendment states explicitly that "[t]he powers not delegated to the United States . . . are reserved to the States." The Court recasts this language to say that the States retain their sovereign powers only to the extent that the Constitution has not divested them of their original powers and transferred those powers to the Federal Government.

This rephrasing is not a distinction without a difference; rather, it reflects the Court's unprecedented view that Congress is free under the Commerce Clause to assume a State's traditional sovereign power, and to do so without judicial review of its action. Indeed, the Court's view of federalism appears to relegate the States to precisely the trivial role that opponents of the Constitution feared they would occupy.....

Although the Court's opinion purports to recognize that the States retain some sovereign power, it does not identify even a single aspect of state authority that would remain when the Commerce Clause is invoked to justify federal regulation. In *Maryland v. Wirtz*, (1968), overruled by *National League of Cities* and today reaffirmed, the Court sustained an extension of the FLSA to certain hospitals, institutions, and schools. Although the Court's opinion in *Wirtz* was comparatively narrow, Justice Douglas, in dissent, wrote presciently that the Court's reading of the Commerce Clause would enable

the National Government [to] devour the essentials of state sovereignty, though that sovereignty is attested by the Tenth Amendment.

Today's decision makes Justice Douglas' fear once again a realistic one.

As I view the Court's decision today as rejecting the basic precepts of our federal system and limiting the constitutional role of judicial review, I dissent.

> *"In our system of government there is reason to view with dismay any decision that makes federalism and the basic rights of the states merely political questions and procedural issues."*

# *Garcia* Affects the Balance of Power in the Federal System

## S. Kenneth Howard

*S. Kenneth Howard, who died in 1985, served as executive director of the U.S. Advisory Commission on Intergovernmental Relations (ACIR). In the following viewpoint, he analyzes the short- and long-term effects of the 1985* Garcia v. San Antonio Metropolitan Transit Authority *decision. The question asked in the case was whether or not Congress violated the Constitution's commerce clause by attempting to enforce the provisions of the Fair Labor Standards Act (FLSA) with respect to employees of San Antonio's publicly owned mass transit system. The Court found that Congress was not overstepping its authority in affording these employees the same wage and hour provisions outlined in the act. Howard maintains that while the short-term effects of the ruling are fiscal and procedural, with accompanying high costs to local governments, he argues they are less significant than the decision's long-range consequences for American federalism.*

S. Kenneth Howard, "A Message from *Garcia*," *Public Administration Review*, vol. 45, Special Issue: Law and Public Affairs, November 1985, pp. 738–41. Copyright © 1985 American Society for Public Administration. Reproduced by permission of Blackwell Publishing Ltd.

The 1985 ruling in *Garcia v. San Antonio Metropolitan Transit Authority* by the U.S. Supreme Court has profound implications for American federalism. At issue in the case was whether the minimum wage and overtime provisions of the national Fair Labor Standards Act (FLSA) apply to employees of publicly owned mass transit systems. In a 1976 case, *National League of Cities v. Usery*, the court had ruled that these provisions did not apply to state and local units "in areas of traditional governmental functions." That decision was the first in many years to give much judicial weight to the Tenth Amendment, which provides that "The powers not delegated to the United States by the Constitution, nor prohibited by it to the States, are reserved to the States respectively, or to the people." The court could have dealt with *Garcia* simply by saying whether or not mass transit was a "traditional" governmental function. Indeed, the [Ronald] Reagan administration had urged that the court rule mass transit *not* a traditional function and simply extend FLSA coverage to include this group of municipal employees. The court, however, went much further and overturned *National League of Cities v. Usery* entirely, and the language of the decision casts great doubt on the current significance of the Tenth Amendment.

Two effects of *Garcia* can be distinguished. First, the ruling has immediate short-run impacts that are mostly fiscal and procedural in character. Second, it has major long-run implications for the nature of the American system of government.

## Immediate Effects

The *Garcia* decision affects the coverage of the Fair Labor Standards Act in 50 states and approximately 3,000 counties, 19,000 municipalities, 17,000 townships, 15,000 school districts, and 29,000 local special districts, employing approximately 7 million persons full time and having aggregate payrolls exceeding $12 billion per month. Given that breadth of coverage, it is very difficult to estimate precisely what actions will be required to comply with the ruling and what they will cost. Many governmental units already comply with FLSA standards; more probably do not; most probably comply in part but what it will take to get their procedures and practices into compliance will vary widely.

A few generalizations can be ventured. First, compliance with the overtime requirements will be more difficult and expensive than compliance with the minimum wage standards. Most full-time employees of most governments are already receiving the minimum wage or more, especially past the entry level.

Second, the fiscal effects of meeting the new standards will probably be more heavily felt among local than state governments. This conclusion says nothing about the relative competence of these two levels or about the quality of their existing personnel practices. It simply recognizes that the functions that are most likely to cause overtime compliance difficulties (fire and police) constitute a far higher proportion of local than of state spending. State governments have few firefighters and their law enforcement personnel (highway patrols, bureaus of investigation, game wardens, and the like) are a relatively small part of total state personnel.

Third, the bulk of the costs and changes will be associated with fire and police activities. The work practices of these fields, especially 24-hour shifts for firefighters, tend to generate work that is defined as overtime under the regulations that now apply. In addition, certain other fields that may generate a lot of overtime work, such as teaching and nursing, are exempted from coverage.

Fourth, the smallest local governments will not be affected. Indeed, governments with fewer than five full-time fire or police officials have been exempted.

Fifth, personnel costs for local governments will rise initially. In the long run, labor market wages may accommodate the new definitions of overtime and how that work is to be compensated. But in the short run, wage levels are set, many by contract, and more rigorous standards for overtime payments can only mean higher costs. Work-shift practices among firefighters provide a ready example of the problem. Under FLSA overtime must be paid to firefighters if they work more than 212 hours over a 28-day period. This standard approximates a 53-hour week, but the most common staffing pattern among cities—24 hours on and 48 hours off—comes out to 56 hours per week.

Sixth, standards based on weighted averages tend least to reflect practices in small and medium-sized communities so that the costs of compliance may be relatively higher in these localities. The 212-hour standard for firefighters was derived by trying to determine the work week practices of local governments, weighting each locality in the final calculations by the number of firefighters employed. This approach is certainly reasonable. But weighting necessarily results in standards reflecting personnel practices in the largest urban centers, jurisdictions which tend to be more heavily unionized. These jurisdictions are the very ones that are more likely to have adapted their current operating practices most closely to FLSA standards. Jurisdictions whose current practices vary most widely from the FLSA standards will face relatively greater compliance costs.

Seventh, to the extent that localities are unable or unwilling to raise revenues to meet higher labor costs, services will be reduced. From an economic viewpoint, this statement is axiomatic: if resources are fixed and you must get more of one thing, you are going to get less of something else. Service reductions are not the only alternative localities can select, nor perhaps even the most likely. But in the short run, they are almost inevitable. They are inevitable due to another characteristic of state and local governments: almost without exception they must balance their spending with their revenues annually. If an event like a court action forces costs to rise and tax rates have already been set, other options are limited. As the 1980–82 recession demonstrated, state and local governments will make service reductions when required to meet the mandate of a balanced budget. These reductions need not come solely from the activities causing the higher costs; they may be spread over the entire range of local activities. Nor need the reductions be permanent, depending on how the locality and the wage market deal with the new costs associated with overtime work.

## Estimated Costs

Although comprehensive cost estimates on a national scale are impossible to provide, some less global estimates have been made and they are worth noting. Two states illustrate the risks encountered in trying to make broad cost generalizations. Maryland chose to implement FLSA standards some years ago voluntarily and officials there anticipate little additional cost as a result of *Garcia*. In contrast, Minnesota initially estimated that its additional costs could run as high as $7.4 million annually.

At the local level, probably the best broad national estimate has been compiled by the International City Management Association, which calculated the additional overtime costs for three groups of employees: firefighters, police, and low-level professionals. It estimates an annual compliance cost of between $321 million and $1.5 billion. This spread of almost 5 to 1 from top to bottom suggests the difficulties of acquiring any reliable numbers on this issue.

None of these estimates reflect the effects of bargaining or market changes, which may drive down pay rates when coming into compliance, or how efficiencies stemming from efforts to reduce overtime hours may reduce costs. Nor do these estimates reflect other factors that may induce higher costs, such as implementing new record systems, paying legal counsel for advice on achieving compliance, court costs, retroactive payments that may be required, and other factors.

Finally, the rather unpredictable swath the decision may cut through local practices and employee preferences can be demonstrated with a few specific illustrations. The new requirements virtually eliminate using compensatory time-off, rather than cash payments for overtime, even if the compensatory time is calculated at a time-and-a-half rate. Some employees prefer the additional time off to cash and accumulate such time for special purposes. But this option has been virtually removed for both employers and employees. In a similar vein, off-duty police officers are often given the opportunity to earn additional money by appearing in uniform at major events, such as football games or rock concerts, to help handle crowds and traffic. Usually the promoter of the event pays the municipality for this help, and it is legally defined as joint employment if a local ordinance requires the use of such officers. However, under FLSA standards, this work will have to be treated as overtime employment by municipalities and compensated at time-and-a-half rates. Police officers note that this increase may cause promoters to propose other arrangements and deny them this opportunity to earn a little extra money.

Even the practices of volunteer fire companies may be affected. These volunteers will have to be paid the minimum wage for all the hours they spend on firefighting activities if local practice provides them with a stipend in excess of their actual expenses. The excess stipend standard currently in the regulations was set some time ago, and it is $2.50 per fire call. Finally, some seasonal employees are exempted, especially in recreational activities such as running ice rinks and outdoor swimming pools. But seasonal employment comes in many shapes and forms. For example, one municipal sewerage district is reducing its sludge pond, as required by a state environmental agency, by applying the sludge to nearby croplands as fertilizer. Most of this material must be applied in April,

May, September, October, and November. During these months, drivers average 10-hour days, six days a week. Until now the drivers had the option of being paid at the overtime rate or having compensatory time calculated at that rate for use during the off-peak months. The new regulations would not permit this practice to continue and will increase the costs of environmental protection as well as disgruntle some employees.

In summary, the coverage of the Fair Labor Standards Act has been altered several times since it was first adopted in 1938 as a progressive legislative measure intended to protect workers from exploitation and to contribute to their well-being. In the opinion of a bare majority of the court, *Garcia* simply made state and local governments face "the same minimum-wage and overtime obligations that hundreds of thousands of other employers, public as well as private, have to meet." But the ruling's immediate effects are widespread and costly. They are also probably less significant than the decision's long-range consequences for American federalism.

## Long-Run Effects

As a precedent, *Garcia* raises serious questions about the underlying character of our federal system. Our Founding Fathers were mindful of the capacity of strong central governments to become tyrannical. To mitigate this possibility, they created a federal system and sought to assure sufficient strength and independence to the component parts so that undue centralization would not occur. Federalism is peculiarly an American contribution to the art of governance, derived from practices settlers found existing among tribes within a single Indian nation.

By design, federalism is dynamic as power ebbs and flows among its constituent parts. But it is intended to be a partnership; to work well, each partner must be strong. By choosing to go well beyond simply extending FLSA coverage to transit workers, the court raised basic constitutional issues about how best to assure and preserve a strong partnership. As the 5-4 vote and the poignant dissents suggest, the issues are not easy ones.

Because local governments are not mentioned in the Constitution, discussions of constitutional issues always focus on the states, which are given constitutional recognition. In American jurisprudence, local governments are legally creatures of the states, deriving their powers from the states themselves or the states' citizens. Consequently, local governments can be no stronger than their source of power, the states, and any action which casts a shadow over the states as *Garcia* does concerns them as well.

For this discussion, the most important issue over which the justices were divided was whether the political power of the states if sufficiently great that judicial power is not required to protect states' rights. Where does the regulatory power of the national government cease and the sovereign power of the states begin? If that determination is made solely through political means and institutions, as contrasted with the courts, how will there be assurance that constitutional limitations will be observed, including the states' reserved powers under the Tenth Amendment?

One can readily empathize with the majority opinion that distinctions between traditional and non-traditional functions of government do not provide an adequate basis for demarcating the boundaries of power. Indeed, the majority felt such standards simply opened the door for judges to decide which policies they liked and which they did not, judgments far better left to elected officials and institutions. The majority contended that there are constitutional limits on federal actions under the Commerce Clause. But those judges saw no need to spell them out in this decision, suggesting subsequent litigation and legislation could be used to establish such limitations. Writing for the majority, Justice [Harry] Blackmun concluded:

> [T]he principle and basic limit on the federal commerce power is that inherent in all congressional action—the built-in restraints that our system provides through state participation in federal government action. The political process ensures that laws that unduly burden the states will not be promulgated.

Practitioners in the vineyards of state government and intergovernmental relations have a very hard time accepting this conclusion on either constitutional or practical grounds. Undeniably senators are elected by states, electoral college votes are cast on a state-by-state basis, and state legislatures define the districts from which we elect members to the House of Representatives. How effective were these forces in restraining Congress when it came to standardizing the drinking age, a determination this nation had left to state discretion and variation since its founding? One need not be a supporter of drunk driving to see only political reasons for such an action, not compelling national interest.

Nor does the existence of federal grant programs establish that the states are as politically effective as the majority opinion suggests. The justices may feel laws do not unduly burden the states, but state and local officials certainly think grant conditions do, and those conditions that have their basis in federal law.

Indeed, there is a widespread feeling that our political practices have changed so much in recent years that state and local governments have less influence in our political processes than ever before. The Advisory Commission on Intergovernmental Relations is currently exploring these issues. Historically, political parties have been rooted in state and local governments and have been bastions for their concerns. However, modern campaign finance techniques and the centralizing and personalizing nature of modern media make today's parties far less effectual than in earlier times. Successful candidates come readily to mind who raise their own money directly, use the media skillfully, and create their own campaign organizations without reference to state or local party apparatus and with only a nod to national party organizations. There is great reason to fear that the persons elected through our current political processes will give little weight to state and local concerns, because structures and persons rooted in those locales often have little significance in determining the electoral success of a particular candidate.

Limitations on the exercise of power must be set out, as the majority opinion argues, but should they be left to the political and electoral institutions to the extent the majority opinion suggests? Justice [Lewis] Powell writing for the dissenters argued that political processes are not the proper means for enforcing constitutional limitations.

> The fact that Congress generally does not transgress constitutional limits on its power to reach State activities does not make judicial review any less necessary to rectify the cases in which it does do so. The States' role in our system of government is a matter of constitutional law, not of legislative grace.

Even more pointedly he noted:

> Despite some genuflecting in Court's opinion to the concept of federalism, today's decision effectively reduces the Tenth Amendment to meaningless rhetoric when Congress acts pursuant to the Commerce Clause.

The Tenth Amendment was not a vote-getting, throw-away provision during the adoption of the Constitution. Much opposition to the Constitution was rooted in the fear that an overly powerful national government would eventually eliminate the states as viable political entities. This concern was voiced repeatedly during the debates over ratification, and proponents of the Constitution had to make assurances that a bill of rights, including a provision explicitly reserving powers to the states, would be among the first business of the new Congress.

In short, in our system of government there is reason to view with dismay any decision that makes federalism and the basic rights of the states merely political questions and procedural issues.

Although *Garcia* generates problems of immediate concern and cost, its greater impact probably lies in how it affects the balance of power in our federal system. The majority opinion places a lot of faith in the self-restraint of Congress. State and local officials who have watched Congress act in such traditionally state and local policy areas as rat control and drinking ages are much less sanguine about the long-run likelihood of congressional self-restraint. However imprecise its language, the Constitution calls for a balance of power between the states and the national government, a balance the courts need to consider and the Founding Fathers thought was essential to protecting our fundamental liberties. It has been the traditional role of the Supreme Court to determine where the imprecise lines are to be drawn and the balances struck. Those who believe in a strong federalism share Justice [William] Rehnquist's hope that these points of principle will again, in time, command the support of a majority of the court.

> "Garcia takes the easy way out. It washes the Court's hands of Tenth Amendment problems and leaves the states to take their complaints to the Congress."

# The Court Ignored the Constitution's Institutional Arrangements for Political Convenience

## A.E. Dick Howard

*A.E. Dick Howard is White Burkett Miller Professor of Law and Public Affairs and Earle K. Shawe Research Professor at the University of Virginia.* In the following viewpoint, he contends that in Garcia v. San Antonio Metropolitan Transit Authority *(1985), the majority turned their backs on federalism and its principles that set limits on Congress's exercise of its powers. The issue in* Garcia *was whether the minimum wage and overtime provisions in the Fair Labor Standards Act (FLSA) applied to state and local governments. The Court ruled that they did, thereby overruling* National League of Cities v. Usery *(1976), which had held that the regulation of the activities of state and local governments in areas of "traditional governmental functions" was a violation of the Tenth Amendment. Howard reinforces the idea that federalism is a key component of the Constitution's institutional arrangement, checking centralized government power and protecting individual rights.*

A.E. Dick Howard, "*Garcia*: Of Federalism and Constitutional Values," *Publius: The Journal of Federalism*, vol. 16, Summer 1986, pp. 17–31. Copyright © 1986 CSF Associates, Inc. Reproduced by permission of the publisher and the author.

A merican federalism has often puzzled foreign visitors to the United States. While Englishmen may talk of devolution for such regions as Scotland, they, like most people outside the American system, have been tutored in traditions of a centralized government in which local affairs are administered by units having no independent existence.

## What Is Federalism?

American federalism is also something of a mystery to many Americans, including, alas, many of our judges. To some observers, federalism means a functional search for convenience and administrative efficiency, for example, the "sorting out" of functions which is the subject of much contemporary debate in Washington, D.C. To others, federalism means "states' rights," an idea that often carries the connotation of parochialism and reaction, perhaps racism and repression.

Legal realists did their part, too, in undermining the notion that federalism has a principled place in the American constitutional order. Federalism is dismissed by some legal thinkers as being either a myth and delusion or, more darkly, an obstacle thrown in the path of progress and social justice.

After the famous "constitutional revolution" of 1937 [during which the Supreme Court upheld the New Deal's social legislation], the justices of the U.S. Supreme Court seemed to turn their backs on arguments that the principles of federalism set limits on the Congress' exercise of its powers to regulate the national economy. Dismissed in 1942 as a "mere truism," the Tenth Amendment was relegated, like the old patent models once stored in the Patent Office, to the nation's jurisprudential attic.

For decades after 1937, law professors schooled generations of law students in the belief that it was inconceivable that the Supreme Court would rediscover the Tenth Amendment or seek, in the name of federalism, to curb the Article I powers of the Congress. This conventional wisdom was upset in 1976 when the Court, in *National League of Cities v. Usery (NLC)* ruled that the Congress, in extending the Fair Labor Standards Act's minimum wage and maximum hour provisions to state and local government employees, had exceeded its constitutional powers.

## From *NLC* to *Garcia*

*NLC* rekindled the debate over the constitutional dimensions of federalism by holding that Congress could not exercise its authority over commerce in such a way as "to directly displace the States' freedom to structure integral operations in areas of traditional governmental functions." But that decision, from which four justices dissented, was only the opening salvo in a constitutional barrage. It required further litigation to discover *NLC*'s scope and meaning.

*NLC* was an embattled opinion from the very beginning. Justice Harry A. Blackmun, who furnished the fifth vote to make up a majority, betrayed his tentative mood. He confessed that he was "not untroubled by certain possible implications in the Court's opinion," but he was willing to go along with the decision's essential thrust. Even so, he read the Court's opinion (written by Justice William H. Rehnquist) as adopting a "balancing" approach, leaving it open for federal action to prevail in the face of a Tenth Amendment objection if the federal interest is "demonstrably greater" and if it is essential that states comply with federal standards.

The subsequent travails of *NLC* are familiar to anyone who has observed how a majority of justices hostile to, or uneasy with, an earlier decision, can reinterpret or confine that precedent until little remains of it. In 1981, in *Hodel v. Virginia Surface Mining & Reclamation, Inc.*, Justice Thurgood Marshall (one of the dissenters in *NLC*) took the language of the 1976 decision and rearranged it into three requirements, *each* of which had to be satisfied before a Tenth Amendment challenge to a congressional act predicated on the commerce clause could succeed in the courts. First, the challenged statute must regulate the "States as States." Second, it must address matters that are "indisputably 'attributes of state sovereignty.'" Third, the states' compliance with the federal law must "directly impair their ability 'to structure integral operations in areas of traditional functions.'" (Note the choice of words like "indisputably" and "directly impair.")

Even if a state could surmount these rigorous standards, Justice Marshall, in a footnote, added yet another hurdle: "There are situations in which the nature of the federal interest advanced may be such that it justifies State submissions." This additional reservation, of course, embodied the thrust of Justice Blackmun's reading of a "balancing" approach in *NLC*.

In [Italian composer Giacomo] Puccini's [opera] *Turandot*, the princess puts three riddles to would-be suitors. If they fail to get the answers right, they are put to death. States attempting to rise to the challenge posed by the three-part *Hodel* test found themselves dispatched like those hapless victims in *Turandot*. In *United Transportation Union v. Long Island Rail Road Company* (1982), the Court applied *Hodel*'s third prong. Operation of a railroad was held not to be an integral part of traditional state activities so as to be immune from federal regulation.

In the *Long Island Rail Road Company* case the Court was unanimous. Two other cases, however, in which Tenth Amendment challenges also failed, showed the depth of the fissures in the Court over the meaning of *NLC*. In *FERC v. Mississippi* (1982), five justices rejected a Tenth Amendment challenge to federal energy legislation requiring state regulatory agencies to decide whether to adopt certain federal standards governing gas and electric utilities and also prescribing procedures for state agencies to follow in evaluating those standards. Justice Blackmun, for the majority, saw the case as essentially a preemption case; that is, the Congress could have preempted state regulation of utilities entirely. Justice Sandra Day O'Connor, in one of her sharpest dissents on the Court, objected to the federal act as operating to "conscript state utility commissions into the national bureaucratic army."

*EEOC v. Wyoming*, decided in 1983, provoked an equally sharp exchange among the justices, who again split five to four. Justice William J. Brennan, Jr. for the majority, upheld the extension of the Age Discrimination in Employment Act to state and local governments. In the *Wyoming* case, a supervisor for the state's game and fish department had complained of his being involuntarily retired at age 55. Brennan conceded that the management of state parks was a "traditional state function." But, invoking *Hodel*'s third requirement, Brennan ruled that the federal act did not "directly impair" the state's ability to "structure integral operations in arenas of traditional governmental operations." The dissenters complained that the majority were doing violence to the constitutional precepts of federalism.

By the time *Garcia v. San Antonio Metropolitan Transit Authority* reached the Court (the same year as *EEOC v. Wyoming* was decided), the principles so boldly declared by Justice Rehnquist only seven years earlier in *NLC* were sorely beleaguered. Justice John Paul Stevens, labeling *NLC* "pure judicial fiat," had called in *EEOC* for its overruling. Even more ominous for *NLC*'s survival was the Court's decision, having heard initial arguments in *Garcia*, to set the case for reargument and to have the parties brief the question: "Whether or not the principles of the Tenth Amendment as set forth in *National League of Cities v. Usery* . . . should be reconsidered?"

This was a cryptic statement. It might have implied that the Court's concern was not necessarily with the underlying notion that there is indeed a Tenth Amendment constraint on the Congress' use of its commerce power but rather with the particular formulation (such as "traditional state function") of that limit in *NLC*. After all, even though the Tenth Amendment argument had failed in the several cases, such as *Hodel*, that had been brought before the Court since *NLC*, in formal terms, at least, the Court had applied a modified *NLC* test (the one formulated in *Hodel*) in most of the cases decided after *NLC*.

As we now know, the Court appears to have had the intention of asking whether *NLC* should be reconsidered. When *Garcia* was decided, in February 1985, Justice Blackmun concluded that in order to protect their interests, the states should look to the "procedural safeguards inherent in the structure of the federal system" rather than to the courts. *NLC*, he said, must therefore be overruled. The hesitant fifth justice in *NLC*, who was "not untroubled" by that decision's implications, had now cast his lot with *NLC*'s dissenters. In *Garcia*, the Court split five to four; the Chief Justice and Justices Powell, Rehnquist, and O'Connor dissented.

In *Garcia*, a federal district court had viewed municipal ownership and operation of a mass transit system as being a traditional state government function. Under *NLC*, therefore, the system was exempt from the minimum-wage and maximum-hour requirements of the Fair Labor Standards Act. Thus, *Garcia* involved the same statute that had been at issue in *NLC*.

For those wanting to bury *NLC*, the path was made easier by the difficulties that lower courts had encountered in trying to decide, case by case, which functions of state or local governments fell within the ambit of the protection afforded by *NLC*. A purely historical approach would not suffice, because that would rule out any recognition of important functions— mass transit being one—which states and localities had taken on in more recent times. Nor did such distinctions as that between "governmental" and "proprietary" functions—a line once drawn in cases involving state immunity from federal taxation—offer much help.

*Garcia* takes the easy way out. It washes the Court's hands of Tenth Amendment problems and leaves the states to take their complaints to the Congress. In reading the majority opinion in *Garcia,* one is reminded of other areas in which the Court has taken an essentially abdicationist approach. A parallel might be drawn to the Court's abandonment of its earlier efforts to find some principled limit to Congress' authority to use its commerce power to regulate the private sector; once the Court had settled, in 1964, upon a "rational basis" test to review commerce clause legislation, it was plain that the Congress had a clear field, unencumbered by any concerns about judicial review. . . .

## The Values of Federalism

No justice is equally sensitive to each and every clause in the Constitution. Justice Hugo L. Black believed in his heart in the First Amendment; indifferent to charges that he was a single-minded absolutist, he incanted, "'Congress shall make no law' means 'Congress shall make no law.'" But it is fair to say that he did not get so fired up about the force of the Fourth Amendment's prohibitions against unreasonable searches and seizures.

*Garcia* reminds us how very differently the justices of the present Court feel about federalism. Those who voted with the majority are not bestirred to find ways to give meaning or force to the Tenth Amendment. For them it has about as much value as a source of judicial standards as does the Gettysburg Address, perhaps even less.

*Garcia*'s dissenters feel very differently. Justice Rehnquist, the author of the Court's opinion in NLC, is well known for having extolled the virtues of federalism and localism in a number of contexts. Dissenting opinions, of course, in federalism cases as in other areas, tend to bring out the strongest expressions of a justice's philosophy. Thus, in her *FERC* dissent, Justice O'Connor praised the innovations that have originated in the states, praised federalism as enhancing the opportunity for all citizens to participate in representative government, and proclaimed federalism to be "a salutary check on governmental power." In his *EEOC* dissent, Chief Justice Warren E. Burger weighed in with a like conclusion: "Nothing in the Constitution permits Congress to force the states into a Procrustean national mold that takes no account of local needs and conditions."

Justice Powell, in his *Garcia* dissent, applied these generalizations to the kinds of services listed in *NLC* (such as police and fire protection and sanitation and public health) as coming under Tenth Amendment protection. They are, he said, "activities that epitomize the concerns of local, democratic government . . . activities engaged in by state and local governments that affect the everyday lives of citizens. These are services that people are in a position to understand and evaluate and, in a democracy, have the right to oversee."

Such statements should not be dismissed as mere value judgments, as statements of policy or personal attitude. Any justice must, in giving life to constitutional provisions, breathe something of the spirit that informs that provision. This is why First Amendment opinions by Justices Oliver Wendell Holmes or Louis D. Brandeis or Hugo Black endure: not merely for analytical insights, but because they surge with an understanding of the principles that the Constitution's framers sought to weave into the constitutional fabric.

Local government can be a school for citizenship. Through participation in local government a citizen can be educated in the civic virtues. In the words of [nineteenth-century French author of *Democracy in America*] Alexis de Tocqueville: the townsperson "practises the art of government in the small sphere within his reach; he . . . collects clear practical notions on the nature of his duties and the extent of his rights." Obeying the sovereign's command, whether it comes from a national assembly or some other source, teaches little about citizenship. It is deliberating together and making choices that is the citizen's classroom.

The case for federalism rests upon a concern for preserving the right of choice. Making choices is the essence of political freedom. In the American constitutional system, the right of individuals to participate in the process of making choices is reinforced by a cluster of fundamental values: free expression, criticism of public officials, equality in representation, the right to vote, access to the ballot. State and local governments have often trampled these very values, for example, in denying the right to vote on grounds of race. The remedies for such abuses lie in vigorous enforcement of constitutional guarantees and in the Congress' exercise of its legislative powers to protect civil rights. But the need to protect individuals against state or local government trespasses does not undermine the conclusion that a healthy federalism can itself operate to enhance opportunities for choice.

Accountability is a key to understanding the importance of federalism. Justice O'Connor made this point most tellingly in her *FERC* dissent. Objecting to federal enlistment of state utility commissions for federal purposes, she said:

> Local citizens hold their utility commissions accountable for the choices they make. Citizens, moreover, understand that legislative authority usually includes the power to decide which issues to debate, as well as which policies to adopt. Congressional compulsion of state agencies, unlike preemption, blurs the lines of political accountability and leaves citizens feeling that their representatives are no longer responsive to local needs.

Chief Justice Burger made a similar point in his dissent in *EEOC v. Wyoming.* Supporting Wyoming's right to decide at what age to retire fish and game employees, he declared:

> If poachers destroy the fish and game reserves of Wyoming, it is not to the Congress that people are going to complain, but to state and local authorities who will have to justify their actions in selecting wardens. Since it is the state that

bears the responsibility for delivering the services, it is clearly an attribute of state sovereignty to choose those who will perform those duties.

Federalism, like other institutional rights, is more than simply good political theory—though it is certainly that as well. Under the U.S. Constitution, institutional rights are a guarantor of individual rights. Even such basic assurances as those in the Bill of Rights and in the Fourteenth Amendment do not secure absolute personal rights. They protect against governmental—that is, against institutional—actions, not against infringements by private parties. Thus if the citizen is to hope for security for individual rights, he or she must be able to count on the institutional safeguards explicit or implicit in the Constitution.

The framers of the U.S. Constitution, whatever their other aims and tasks, had to create a frame of government. They built certain institutional arrangements into the very core of the Constitution, such as the separation of powers and federalism. Today's citizen—as heir to the system thus created—has a fundamental entitlement to live under the system of government spelled out in the Constitution. From time to time, the structure thus created can prove inconvenient. Yet it is not, on that account, to be abandoned, as the Supreme Court made clear in reviewing the constitutionality of the legislative veto.

Federalism was a natural principle to a people who had recently fought a war against England to secure the right to make local decisions about local matters. Moreover, the securing of the states' inherent place in the Union was a necessary commitment for the Federalists to get the Constitution underway. The Constitution appealed to many of those who were concerned that there be devices to arrest any undue concentration of power. From the beginning, therefore, federalism became a linchpin of the constitutional order.

One of the striking phenomena of the modern Supreme Court has been its heightened concern for enforcing the guarantees of the Bill of Rights. There is, of course, much room for debate among the justices as to the scope and meaning of many of those constitutional provisions. One would be surprised to read, however, in any Supreme Court opinion, a call for the justices to step aside from their judicial role and leave implementation and enforcement of the Bill of Rights to the Congress and the states.

Yet the *Garcia* majority refused to enforce the Tenth Amendment. For those who view *Garcia* with concern, who see a link between federalism and constitutionalism, between federalism and individual rights, what can one say of the future?

## *Garcia* Was a Mistake

Near the end of his *Garcia* opinion, Justice Blackmun summed up the Court's basic thesis: "The political process ensures that the laws that unduly burden the States will not be promulgated." In the factual setting presented in *Garcia*, Blackmun found that "the internal safeguards of the political process have performed as intended."

What proof might the Court entertain to demonstrate that the "internal safeguards" had not, on the facts of another case, performed as intended? What empirical data might be relevant to such an inquiry? What level of proof would be required? How important to a state must a threatened interest be? How serious a threat must be posed by the failure of the internal safeguards?

On such questions we must speculate. Justice Blackmun, in *Garcia*, said that the Court was not, in that case, required "to identify or define what affirmative limits the constitutional structure might impose on federal action affecting the States under the Commerce Clause." Understandably, Justice Powell, who in a footnote in his dissent noted the majority's seeming qualification of its otherwise abdicationist opinion, found himself unenlightened as to just what was meant.

The states may want to use future cases as the occasion to explore whether, indeed, the Court has left the field entirely and unequivocally to the Congress or whether there might still be some Tenth Amendment restraints on the Congress. Given Justice Blackmun's criticisms of *NLC*, one presumes that, to attract his vote, a litigant invoking the Tenth Amendment would not only have to show an egregious failure of the political safeguards of federalism but also advance a tidier set of standards than those which Blackmun found in *NLC*, or anywhere else in existing case law.

There are, of course, many other opportunities, quite apart from Tenth Amendment cases, for the Court to vindicate the values of federalism. The Eleventh Amendment survives, as suggested in the *Atascadero* case decided a few months after *Garcia*. There are frequent opportunities to interpret federal statutes in light of their effects on state and local governments. The Court's 1981 *Pennhurst* decision, for example, laid down the salutary principle that federal grant conditions, to be binding on state and local governments, must be clearly identified as such when grant funds are accepted. Comity, a handmaiden of federalism, can be invoked when reviewing lower court uses of their equity powers in cases involving state institutions (such as prisons) or when restraining a federal court's intervention in state court proceedings.

As for *Garcia*, no opinion is graven in stone. Least of all need one assume the immutability of a five-to-four opinion reached over strong dissents, overturning such a recent precedent, and raising not some transient question of statutory interpretation but a fundamental question touching an enduring constitutional principle.

One would, however, be rash to predict early and outright reversal of *Garcia*, even assuming new appointments to the Supreme Court. Justice Blackmun's overruling of *NLC* was made easier by the erosion of that decision in such sequels as *EEOC v. Wyoming* and *FERC v. Mississippi*. Likewise, to undermine and overthrow *Garcia* may take patience as well as, of course, favorable factual situations and effective advocacy.

One hopes that a majority of the justices will come to view *Garcia* as a mistake. Federalism, as one of the intrinsic components of the constitutional system, should no more be consigned to the discretion of the legislative branch than should the rest of the Constitution. It may well be that, when the Tenth Amendment is invoked, the Court should be slow to step in and displace congressional judgment. But to husband judicial resources is not the same thing as renouncing them altogether, as *Garcia* seems to invite.

An old principle in American jurisprudence is that no branch of government should be the ultimate and unfettered judge of its own powers. One of the finest hours in modern constitutional law came when the Court called a president to account in *United States v. Nixon* (1974). *Garcia* is no mere case about overtime for bus drivers; it has implications for the rule of law. A Court that concerns itself with enforcing the Constitution and ensuring the protection of individuals should not neglect federalism. Federalism, too, is part of the constitutional plan and a buttress of individual liberties.

> *"It surely stretches the imagination to argue that requiring states to pay their employees time-and-a-half for work in excess of forty hours per week, as all other employers must, will destroy state sovereignty."*

# Granting Overtime Pay Does Not Destroy State Sovereignty

*Gary Steven Wigodsky*

*Gary Steven Wigodsky practices law in Los Angeles. In the following viewpoint, he argues against the views of the four dissenting justices in* Garcia v. San Antonio Metropolitan Transit Authority *(1985). The Court in that case ruled that Congress has the power under the commerce clause to extend the Fair Labor Standards Act (FLSA), which requires employers to guarantee minimum wage and overtime pay to their employees, to state and local governments. Wigodsky maintains that the minority justices had very little constitutional support for their positions but rather based their objections on a historical vision of state sovereignty.*

The *Garcia* majority based its decision not on the supposition that state sovereignty, which *National League of Cities* sought to preserve, should not be protected. Rather, the Court ruled that the political process is both the constitutionally mandated and realistically most practical place for federalism to be preserved. Accordingly, the Court ruled that Congress's

Gary Steven Wigodsky, "The Supreme Court Overrules *National League of Cities v. Usery*, Thereby Extending the Fair Labor Standards Act to Virtually All State and Local Government Employees," *Boston College Law Review*, vol. 27, December 1985, pp. 144–48. Copyright © 1985 by Boston College Law School. Reproduced by permission.

power under the commerce clause is not impliedly limited by the tenth amendment's embodiment of federalism or state sovereignty. As a result, the Court held that the minimum wage and overtime provisions of the FLSA [Fair Labor Standards Act] are applicable to SAMTA [San Antonio Metropolitan Transit Authority] employees, as well as to all other state and local government employees.

## The Dissenters' View of Federalism

Justice [Lewis] Powell, writing for all four Justices in dissent, argued first that the Court had no justification for straying from stare decisis [precedent] by overruling *National League of Cities*, a recent precedent on which all members of the Court had previously relied. He went on to argue that the reason the majority found *National League of Cities* unworkable was because it mischaracterized the decision as requiring the Court to define the scope of traditional state functions. Justice Powell argued, on the other hand, that as Justice [Harry] Blackmun had noted in his concurrence in *National League of Cities*, the tenth amendment's reservation of rights to the states requires the Court to balance the federal interests with the interests of state sovereignty, a task in which the Court often engages. Most importantly, therefore, Justice Powell argued that the Court had eviscerated the American scheme of federalism by relegating it to the political process, thereby stripping it of its constitutional might as enforced by judicial review.

The view of federalism taken by the four dissenters was an historical one. They first argued that the ratification of the Constitution was the result of a compromise between federalists and anti-federalists which specifically reserved for the states, in the tenth amendment, all powers not explicitly delegated to the federal government. The dissenters therefore concluded that the Court had emasculated the sovereignty of the states by relegating it to the political whim of Congress, and then shielding that exercise of political power from constitutional judicial review. Finally, reiterating that the Court's role should have been to balance the federal and state interests involved, as five Justices had done in *National League of Cities*, the dissent concluded that the application of minimum wage and overtime standards to the states obviously endangered the ability of the states to function effectively as sovereigns, while serving no countervailing federal interest.

*Garcia* is the result of one Justice, Justice Blackmun, changing his mind. With the switch of only one Justice, therefore, the Court was as severely split in *Garcia* as it had been in *National League of Cities*. Justice Powell's harsh dissent in *Garcia*, joined by the Chief Justice and Justices [William] Rehnquist and [Sandra Day] O'Connor, accused the Court of altering two hundred years of the constitutional doctrine of federalism. Justice O'Connor also filed a dissent, joined by Justices Powell and Rehnquist, in which she accused the Court of severely violating the spirit of federalism as embodied in the tenth amendment. Both she and Justice Rehnquist, in his own dissenting statement, took the ominous stance that the Court, perhaps with soon to be appointed new Justices, would surely return to the *National League of Cities* doctrine in the future.

## Unworkability of *National League of Cities*

The harsh dissents notwithstanding, the majority in *Garcia* reached the correct result. The Court was persuasive in arguing that *National League of Cities* was neither a practical decision, nor one faithful to the constitutional interests it sought to advance. Despite Justice O'Connor's charge that it had sounded a retreat from the important battle over the vitality of federalism, the Court, in reality, set aside ideological biases and exposed an unworkable and unprincipled decision for what it was. It surely stretches the imagination to argue that requiring states to pay their employees time-and-a-half for work in excess of forty hours per week, as all other employers must, will destroy state sovereignty.

In first finding the *National League of Cities* doctrine unworkable, the Court accurately pointed out the troublesome nature of its endeavor to distinguish between traditional and nontraditional state governmental functions. For example, the Court illustrated the hopelessness in trying to devise a rule which would reconcile the placing by courts of state regulation of drivers on the traditional side, and state regulation of traffic on the nontraditional side. The Court did not, however, overrule recent precedent merely because the rule was difficult to apply. Rather, the Court looked to the factors which made the rule impractical, and correctly found that the major reason was that the rule lacked proper constitutional foundation from the start.

As the Court elucidated, the Constitution provides ample channels in federal elections and in the constitutional amendment process for a state to champion its status as a limited sovereign government under the American system of federalism. The Constitution does not, moreover, make the distinction between federal regulatory power over traditional, as opposed to nontraditional, state functions. Nor does the commerce clause so much as imply Congress's regulatory power is in any way limited by notions of state sovereignty. Moreover, the tenth amendment, by its own terms, reserves for the states only those powers not granted to the federal government, unlike the expressly enumerated power to regulate interstate commerce. The Court's decision in *Garcia*, therefore, is both pragmatically and constitutionally sound. Consequently, state and federal employees should feel secure in their rights under federal labor laws. And federalism still thrives, as enforced by the structure of the American democratic process rather than by the federal courts.

## Ideological Admonitions of the Dissenters

The dissenters in *Garcia*, though no less vehement than the majority, mustered little in the way of specific *constitutional* support for their propositions. Aside from their own historical vision of state sovereignty, the dissenters relied solely on the ambiguous reservations of rights to the states and to the people in the tenth amendment. They did not, however, explain how the tenth amendment's reservation to the states of those powers *"not delegated by the Constitution* [to the federal government]*"* shields the states from congressional regulation under the Constitution's clear delegation of power to Congress to regulate interstate commerce.

Ironically, Justice O'Connor, in her bitter dissent, joined by her fellow strict constructionists on the Court, Justices Powell and Rehnquist, argued that the Court in *Garcia* violated the *"spirit"* of the tenth amendment. Justice Powell, no less caustic in his dissent, attacked the Court for its willingness to defy stare decisis by overturning such a recent decision, even though *National League of Cities* itself was an identical repudiation of the recent precedent set down in *Wirtz* [*v. Maryland*]. Moreover, it seems impossible to reconcile this uneasiness with straying from stare decisis with the dissenters' desire and prediction that *Garcia* will soon be overturned. The dissents, short on persuasive constitutional support, are replete with ideological admonitions that the federal government continues to run rampant over the sovereignty of state governments.

If logical reasoning provides for lasting judicial doctrines, state and local employees will undoubtedly remain protected by the FLSA. If, on the other hand, the ideological battle over states' rights and federal regulatory power continues to rage in the Supreme Court, the dissenters' prediction of a future majority returning to the *National League of Cities* doctrine may well serve once again to deny state workers their rights under the FLSA. In any event, for now, state employees need not worry about states, as their employers, seeking to deny them federally mandated labor protections by claiming that the tenth amendment somehow immunizes states from abiding by federal regulation under the commerce clause. Since Congress's power under the commerce clause is plenary, it seems highly unlikely that states will find any way to circumvent the employee protections of the FLSA, short of relying on a shift in the Supreme Court's composition.

In sum, *Garcia* overrules *National League of Cities*, and with it, the notion that some state employees are not protected by the Fair Labor Standards Act. The *National League of Cities* doctrine had immunized states, engaged in commerce in areas of traditional state functions, from federal labor laws passed by Congress pursuant to the commerce clause of the Constitution. The *Garcia* Court found this doctrine both unworkable and constitutionally unsupportable, though it found that the notion of federalism, purportedly underlying the *National League of Cities* reasoning, alive and well in the structure of the federal government and in the political process, rather than in the tenth amendment. Thus, the states will now have to turn exclusively to the political process, and not to the courts, to fight their battles over federal regulation that they deem injurious to their ability to function as sovereigns. That the states have secured mixed results in convincing Congress to exempt them from some, but not other, federal labor laws displays, as the Court reasoned, that the balancing needed to sustain the American system of federalism is, in fact, successfully occurring in the political process.

A four Justice dissent, however, refused to accept the notion that federalism is a political process, rather than constitutional dogma. Should an opening on the Court present itself, therefore, the desire of the dissenters to return to a tenth amendment limitation on Congress's commerce power may again remove the protections of the Fair Labor Standards Act, in the name of state sovereignty, from many state and local governmental employees.

# Organizations to Contact

*The editors have compiled the following list of organizations concerned with the issues debated in this book. The descriptions are derived from materials provided by the organizations. All have publications or information available for interested readers. The list was compiled on the date of publication of the present volume; the information provided here may change. Be aware that many organizations take several weeks or longer to respond to inquiries, so allow as much time as possible.*

**Advocates for Self-Government**
1010 N. Tennessee Street, Suite 215, Cartersville, GA   30120
(800) 932-1776
Web site: www.theadvocates.org

The Advocates for Self-Government is a nonprofit, nonpartisan libertarian educational organization. Its Web site includes information about its opposition to minimum wage. The organization states that the only "fair" or "correct" wage is what an employer and employee voluntarily agree upon, and it calls for a repeal of the minimum wage law. Its publications include the magazine *The Libertarian Communicator* and the biweekly e-newsletter *The Liberator Online*.

**The American Federation of Labor and Congress of Industrial Organizations (AFL-CIO)**
815 Sixteenth Street NW, Washington, DC   20006
Web site: www.aflcio.org

The American Federation of Labor and Congress of Industrial Organizations (AFL-CIO) was created in 1955 by the merger of the American Federation of Labor and the Congress of Industrial Organizations. The voluntary federation of fifty-six national and international labor unions represents 11 million members. The mission of the AFL-CIO is to improve the lives of working families by building and changing the American labor movement. Its Web site contains fact sheets about the minimum wage as well as a downloadable handbook on raising the minimum wage.

## Association of Community Organizations for Reform Now (ACORN)
739 Eighth Street SE, Washington, DC   20003
(877) 55-ACORN
Web site: www.acorn.org

The Association of Community Organizations for Reform Now (ACORN) is the United States' largest community organization of low- and moderate-income families, working for social justice and stronger communities. ACORN campaigns for better housing, schools, neighborhood safety, health care, job conditions, and more. ACORN has been especially active in leading campaigns to raise the minimum wage. ACORN publishes numerous reports and a biweekly e-newsletter.

## Employment Policies Institute (EPI)
1090 Vermont Ave. NW, Suite 800, Washington, DC   20005
(202) 463-7650 ext. 109
Web site: www.epionline.org

The Employment Policies Institute (EPI) is a nonprofit research organization dedicated to studying public policy issues surrounding employment growth. In particular, EPI focuses on issues that affect entry-level employment, which includes the minimum wage. Among other issues, EPI research has quantified the impact of new labor costs on job creation, explored the connection between entry-level employment and welfare reform, and analyzed the demographic distribution of mandated benefits. The EPI Web site contains links to many articles on the minimum wage.

## The Heritage Foundation
214 Massachusetts Ave. NE, Washington, DC   20002-4999
(202) 546-4400 • fax: (202) 546-8328

Web site: www.heritage.org

The Heritage Foundation is the nation's most broadly supported public policy research institute, with more than 410,000 individual, foundation, and corporate donors. Its mission is to formulate and promote conservative public policies based on the principles of free enterprise, limited government, individual freedom, traditional American values, and a strong national defense. Its Web site includes information on its opposition to the minimum wage.

**Let Justice Roll**
PO Box 2441, Little Rock, AR   72203
(216) 712-4457
e-mail: paulsherry@letjusticeroll.org
Web site: www.letjusticeroll.org

The Let Justice Roll Living Wage Campaign is a nonpartisan coalition of more than ninety faith, community, labor, and business organizations committed to raising the minimum wage. Let Justice Roll organizes at the federal level and in selected states to raise the minimum wage. It conducts Living Wage Days events and an ongoing educational program to inform people of the severity of conditions facing low-wage working people and mobilize support for constructive change. The report *A Just Minimum Wage: Good for Workers, Business, and Our Future* is available on its Web site.

**National League of Cities** (NLC)
1301 Pennsylvania Ave. NW, Suite 550
Washington, DC   20004
(202) 626-3000
e-mail: info@nlc.org
Web site: www.nlc.org

The National League of Cities (NLC) is the oldest and largest national organization representing municipal governments throughout the United States. Its mission is to strengthen and promote cities as centers of opportunity, leadership, and governance. Working in partnership with the forty-nine state municipal leagues, the National League of Cities serves as a resource to and an advocate for the more than nineteen thousand cities, villages, and towns it represents. More than sixteen hundred municipalities of all sizes pay dues to NLC and actively participate as leaders and voting members in the organization. *Nation's Cities Weekly* is NLC's official publication.

## U.S. Department of Labor (DOL)
Frances Perkins Bldg., Washington, DC   20210
(866) 4-USA-DOL
Web site: www.dol.gov

The mission of the Department of Labor (DOL) is to serve and protect American workers, prepare them for new and better jobs, and ensure the adequacy of America's workplaces. In serving and protecting workers, the Department of Labor ensures workers' rights, inspects work sites, shields workers from employment discrimination, administers unemployment insurance programs, collects and analyzes economic data, protects pension benefits, and enforces worker's compensation and wage standards. The Wage and Hour Division of the DOL enforces federal minimum wage, overtime pay, recordkeeping, and child labor requirements of the Fair Labor Standards Act.

# For Further Research

## Books

Irving Bernstein, *A Caring Society: The New Deal, the Worker, and the Great Depression*. Boston: Houghton Mifflin, 1985.

David Card and Alan B. Krueger, *Myth and Measurement: The New Economics of the Minimum Wage*. Princeton, NJ: Princeton University Press, 1997.

Sue Davis, *Justice Rehnquist and the Constitution*. Princeton, NJ: Princeton University Press, 1989.

Barbara Ehrenreich, *Nickel and Dimed: On (Not) Getting By in America*. New York: Metropolitan Books, 2001.

Burton W. Folsom Jr., *New Deal or Raw Deal? How FDR's Economic Legacy Has Damaged America*. New York: Threshold Editions, 2008.

Leslie Friedman, *The Constitutional Rights of Women*. Rev. ed. Madison: University of Wisconsin Press, 1989.

Vivien Hart, *Bound by Our Constitution: Women, Workers, and the Minimum Wage*. Princeton, NJ: Princeton University Press, 1994.

Peter H. Irons and Howard Zinn, *A People's History of the Supreme Court: The Men and Women Whose Cases and Decisions Have Shaped Our Constitution*. New York: Penguin, 2000.

Ellen C. Kearns and Monica Gallagher, *The Fair Labor Standards Act*. Washington, DC: BNA Books, 1999.

Sar A. Levitan and Richard S. Belous, *More than Subsistence: Minimum Wages for the Working Poor*. Baltimore, MD: Johns Hopkins University Press, 1979.

Marc Linder, *"Moments Are the Elements of Profit": Overtime and the Deregulation of Working Hours Under the Fair Labor Standards Act.* Iowa City, IA: Fanpìhuà Press, 2000.

David Neumark and William Wascher, *Minimum Wages.* Cambridge, MA: MIT Press, 2008.

Julie Novkov, *Constituting Workers, Protecting Women: Gender, Law, and Labor in the Progressive Era and New Deal Years.* Ann Arbor: University of Michigan Press, 2001.

Robert Polli et al., *A Measure of Fairness: The Economics of Living Wages and Minimum Wages in the United States.* Ithaca, NY: ILR Press, 2008.

Simon Rottenberg, ed., *The Economics of Legal Minimum Wages.* Washington, DC: American Enterprise Institute, 1981.

Burt Solomon, *FDR v. The Constitution: The Court-Packing Fight and the Triumph of Democracy.* New York: Walker, 2006.

Jerold L. Waltman, *The Politics of the Minimum Wage.* Champaign: University of Illinois Press, 2000.

## Periodicals

Gretchen Agena, "What's So 'Fair' About It? The Need to Amend the Fair Labor Standards Act," *Houston Law Review*, Winter 2002.

Zoe Baird, "State Empowerment After *Garcia*," *Urban Lawyer*, Summer 1986.

J.M. Balkin, "Ideology and Counter-Ideology from *Lochner* to *Garcia*," *UMKC Law Review*, Winter 1986.

Sotirios A. Barber, *"National League of Cities v. Usery*: New Meaning for the Tenth Amendment?" *Supreme Court Review*, 1976.

Craig Becker and Paul Strauss, "Representing Low-Wage Workers in the Absence of a Class: The Peculiar Case of Section 16 of the Fair Labor Standards Act and the Underenforcement of Minimum Labor Standards," *Minnesota Law Review*, May 2008.

Gregory A. Caldeira, "Public Opinion and the U.S. Supreme Court: FDR's Court Packing Plan," *American Political Science Review*, December 1987.

William R. Denny, "Breakdown of the Political Safeguards of Federalism: A Response to *Garcia v. San Antonio Metropolitan Transit Authority*," *Journal of Law & Politics*, Spring 1987.

Irving Dilliard, "A Supreme Court Majority? The Court and Minimum-Wage Legislation," *Harper's Magazine*, November 1936.

Martha A. Field, "*Garcia v. San Antonio Metropolitan Transit Authority*: The Demise of a Misguided Doctrine," *Harvard Law Review*, November 1985.

John Foley, "Questioning the Merits of Federal Minimum Wage Legislation," *Georgetown Journal of Law & Public Policy*, Summer 2007.

Susan L. Gordon, "*New York v. United States*: On the Road Back to *National League of Cities* and Substantive Limits on Congress's Commerce Clause Power," *Journal of Energy, Natural Resources & Environmental Law*, vol. 14, 1994.

Jacob G. Hornberger, "Economic Liberty and the Constitution, Part 12: The Minimum Wage Case," *Freedom Daily*, May 2003.

William E. Leuchtenburg, "F.D.R.'s Court-Packing Plan: A Second Life, a Second Death," *Supreme Court Historical Society Yearbook*, 1988.

Joseph M. Lynch, *"Garcia v. San Antonio Metropolitan Transit Authority*: An Alternate Opinion," *Seton Hall Law Review*, Winter 1986.

Earl M. Maltz, "The Impact of the Constitutional Revolution of 1937 on the Dormant Commerce Clause: A Case Study in the Decline of State Autonomy," *Harvard Journal of Law & Public Policy*, Fall 1995.

Stephanie Mencimer, "Take a Hike: Minimum Wage & Welfare Reform," *New Republic*, May 23, 1994.

Frank I. Michelman, "States' Rights and States' Roles: Permutations of 'Sovereignty' in *National League of Cities v. Usery*," *Yale Law Journal*, May 1977.

William Mishler and Reginald S. Sheehan, "The Supreme Court as a Countermajoritarian Institution? The Impact of Public Opinion on Supreme Court Decisions," *American Political Science Review*, March 1993.

David Neumark and William Wascher, "Minimum Wages and Low-Wage Workers: How Well Does Reality Match the Rhetoric? (Symposium: The Low-Wage Worker: Legal Rights—Legal Realities)," *Minnesota Law Review*, May 2008.

Lee T. Paterson and Coleman J. Walsh Jr., "New Controversy over the Tenth and Eleventh Amendments; the *Garcia* Decision: Has the Supreme Court Placed Local Governments at the Mercy of Congress by Overruling a Nine Year Old Precedent?" *Los Angeles Lawyer*, December 1985.

Franklin D. Roosevelt, "The 'Four Freedoms,'" Annual Message to Congress, January 6, 1941.

Catherine K. Ruckelshaus, "Labor's Wage War," *Fordham Urban Law Journal*, February 2008.

Bernard Schwartz, *"National League of Cities* Again—R.I.P. or a Ghost That Still Walks?" *Fordham Law Review*, November 1985.

Russell S. Sobel, "Theory and Evidence on the Political Economy of the Minimum Wage," *Journal of Political Economy*, August 1999.

Robert L. Stern, "The Court-Packing Plan and the Commerce Clause," *Supreme Court Historical Society Yearbook*, 1988.

Cass R. Sunstein, "*Lochner*'s Legacy," *Columbia Law Review*, June 1987.

Carol Lynn Tebben, "Is Federalism a Political Question? An Application of the Marshallian Framework to *Garcia*," *Publius*, Winter 1990.

Mark Tushnet, "Why the Supreme Court Overruled *National League of Cities*," *Vanderbilt Law Review*, vol. 47, 1994.

Bryan H. Wildenthal, "Judicial Philosophies in Collision: Justice Blackmun, *Garcia*, and the Tenth Amendment," *Arizona Law Review*, Fall 1990.

George F. Will, "The Right Minimum Wage," *Washington Post*, January 4, 2007.

D. Mark Wilson, "Increasing the Mandated Minimum Wage: Who Pays the Price?" *Heritage Foundation Backgrounder*, no. 1162, 1998.

# Index